The Decline of US Labor Unions and the Role of Trade

The Decline of US Labor Unions and the Role of Trade

Robert E. Baldwin

Institute for International Economics
Washington, DC
June 2003

Robert Baldwin, visiting fellow, is Hilldale Professor of Economics Emeritus at the University of Wisconsin–Madison. He was chief economist in the Office of the US Trade Representative (1963–64) and served as a consultant on trade matters in the US Department of Labor (1975–76), the United Nations Conference on Trade and Development (1975), the World Bank (1978–79), and the Organization for Economic Cooperation and Development (1988, 1993, and 1997). From 1991 to 1992, he served as chair of the Panel on Foreign Trade Statistics for the National Academy of Science's Committee on National Trade Statistics. He is a research associate at the National Bureau of Economic Research and a fellow of the American Academy of Arts and Sciences. He was also a member of the external advisory group to Mike Moore, former director-general of the World Trade Organization. He has published numerous theoretical, empirical, and policy-oriented articles in various professional journals in international trade and economic development. Among his books are *Economic Development and Growth* (1966), *Nontariff Distortions of International Trade* (1970), *Foreign Trade Regimes and Economic Development: The Philippines* (1975), *The Political Economy of U.S. Import Policy* (1985), *The Political Economy of U.S.–Taiwan Trade Relations* (1995), and *Congressional Trade Votes: From NAFTA Approval to Fast-Track Defeat* (2000).

INSTITUTE FOR INTERNATIONAL ECONOMICS
1750 Massachusetts Avenue, NW
Washington, DC 20036-1903
(202) 328-9000 FAX: (202) 659-3225
www.iie.com

C. Fred Bergsten, *Director*
Valerie Norville, *Director of Publications and Web Development*
Brett Kitchen, *Director of Marketing and Foreign Rights*

Typesetting by Sandra F. Watts
Printing by Kirby Lithographic Company, Inc.
Cover photo: Terry Vine/Getty Images

Printed in the United States of America
05 04 03   5 4 3 2 1

Library of Congress Cataloging-in-Publication Data

Baldwin, Robert E.
    The decline of US labor unions and the role of trade / Robert E. Baldwin.
       p. cm.
    Includes bibliographical references and index.
    ISBN 0-88132-341-1
    1. Labor unions—United States.
    2. Industrial relations—United States.
    3. International trade.   I. Title

HD6508 .B297 2002
331.88'0973-dc21   2002032237

Contents

Tables

Preface

The Institute has been conducting a wide-ranging Globalization Balance Sheet (GBS) project over the past three years to assess the impact of that phenomenon on the economy and society of the United States. Previous releases have included Lori Kletzer's *Job Loss from Imports: Measuring the Costs,* which addressed the effects of globalization on American jobs and wages; J. David Richardson and Howard Lewis's *Why Global Commitment Really Matters!* which studied the implications for American firms, workers, and communities; and Kenneth Scheve and Matthew Slaughter's *Globalization and the Perceptions of American Workers* on public attitudes toward globalization and their policy implications.

The full GBS series will include a wide-ranging set of studies that measure the underappreciated and underquantified gains and losses from globalization to different groups within the United States, as well as its overall net impact on the country. As a result of these analyses, we hope we will be better able to assess the claims of both proponents and opponents of globalization. More directly, we will be much better situated to address the real losses that can result from the process of increasing global integration. The GBS series is being managed by Senior Fellow J. David Richardson, who has played a major role in the preparation of this volume as he has in all of the other components of the project.

This volume considers the role of increasing economic interdependence in the evolution over recent decades of American trade unions, one of the most active participants in the policy debate on globalization. It seeks to understand whether actual events justify the sometimes skeptical position that the unions have frequently taken (although they have also forged innovative new positions on immigration and exchange-rate misalignment). The study proceeds by assessing the extent to which imports and exports (with international investment and outsourcing in the background) explain the declines, among basically and more-skilled union members, in union membership and in the wage premium that union members have traditionally enjoyed. The study thus complements our earlier work on the impact of globalization on workers themselves. In fact, it has a similar lesson: global competition does contribute modestly to American deunionization, but its effects are far smaller than effects that can be interpreted as increased employer, worker, and legislative resistance to unions. It also has similar policy implications to our earlier work: American workers need better training, education, and insurance—such as the wage insurance recommended by Kletzer—to better engage foreign competition and share in the gains it brings to the overall American economy, as documented by Lewis and Richardson. Only then, as Scheve and Slaughter show, will a majority of American voters approve of more open trade—improved labor adjustment policies are the key. All this material will be integrated with the conclusions of other Globalization Balance Sheet publications in Richardson's upcoming capstone book on the overall project.

The Institute for International Economics is a private nonprofit institution for the study and discussion of international economic policy. Its purpose is to analyze important issues in that area and to develop and communicate practical new approaches for dealing with them. The Institute is completely nonpartisan.

The Institute is funded largely by philanthropic foundations. Major institutional grants are now being received from the William M. Keck, Jr. Foundation and the Starr Foundation. A number of other foundations and private corporations contribute to the highly diversified financial resources of the Institute. Partial funding for the Institute's Globalization Balance Sheet series is being provided by the Toyota Motor Corporation in light of the great interest in these issues in both the United States and Japan. The Andrew W. Mellon Foundation is also supporting these studies. About 31 percent of the Institute's resources in our latest fiscal year were provided by contributors outside the United States, including about 18 percent from Japan.

The Board of Directors bears overall responsibilities for the Institute and gives general guidance and approval to its research program, including the identification of topics that are likely to become important over the medium run (one to three years), and which should be addressed by the Institute. The Director, working closely with the staff and outside Advisory Committee, is responsible for the development of particular projects and makes the final decision to publish an individual study.

The Institute hopes that its studies and other activities will contribute to building a stronger foundation for international economic policy around the world. We invite readers of these publications to let us know how they think we can best accomplish this objective.

C. FRED BERGSTEN
Director
May 2003

Acknowledgments

A number of individuals have provided invaluable assistance in this undertaking. I would first like to thank C. Fred Bergsten for giving me the opportunity to spend short periods at the Institute for International Economics working on the manuscript and interacting with the full-time staff. Presenting preliminary versions of one's work at an Institute working luncheon is a stimulating and rewarding experience at which many very helpful suggestions are received. I am especially grateful for the comments received from Fred Bergsten, Kimberly Elliott, Edward Graham, Gary Hufbauer, Catherine Mann, Marcus Noland, Adam Posen, and Jeffrey Schott. Most of all, I am indebted to J. David Richardson, who manages the Institute's Globalization Balance Sheet series. Dave read both an earlier and final version of the study, making many highly valuable suggestions on methodology, interpretation of results, and readability of the text and tables. Others who read drafts of the manuscript and made very useful suggestions are Matthew Slaughter, Kimberly Elliott, Gary Hufbauer, Robert Lawrence, Fred Bergsten, and two anonymous individuals. I would also like to thank the publications staff at the Institute for their editorial assistance. Finally, I am very grateful to my research assistants at the University of Wisconsin-Madison for helping to assemble the database used in the study. These individuals include Tom Worth, Stephen Yeaple, Meredith Crowley, and Xenia Matchke.

Overview

The American labor movement did not fare well during the last quarter of the 20th century. Not only did the share of workers who were union members fall from 25 percent in 1977 to 14 percent by 1997 (a decline of 44 percent), but the total number of union members also decreased by nearly 4 million between these years despite an overall increase in the number of jobs by more than 37 million.[1] The extent of deunionization in the manufacturing sector was particularly dramatic, with the proportion of unionized workers falling from 38 percent in 1977 to 18 percent in 1997 (a decline of 53 percent).[2] The only bright spot was in the public sector, where the proportion of unionized workers increased.

Various explanations have been set forth to account for this deunionization trend in the private sector. In an article in a symposium on public

---

1. The proportion of union members across industries is from the Current Population Surveys (CPSs) of the US Census Bureau for these years, whereas industry employment figures are from the Office of Employment Projections of the US Bureau of Labor Statistics. The CPS defines a union member as a person who belongs to a labor union or employee association similar to a union. A question on union membership was first included in the annual CPS in 1973, but these data are not comparable with the 1977 and later unionization figures, because the phrase "or employee association" was not added until 1976. See appendix A for a complete description of the data utilized in this study.

2. The decline in unionization during the 1977–87 decade was particularly severe. During this period, the number of union workers in manufacturing declined by 2.6 million, compared with a decline of 1.2 million in the 1987–97 period. The number of nonunion manufacturing jobs increased by 1.8 million in both the 1977–87 and 1987–97 periods.

and private unionization, Melvin Reder (1988) lists the following as the main causal factors cited by various researchers: (1) increased interarea competition, both domestic and international; (2) more rapid growth in certain categories of the labor force (e.g., women, southerners, white-collar workers) that are less favorable to unionization than others; (3) deregulation of transportation industries; (4) declining efforts of unions to recruit new members; (5) government activity that substitutes for union services (e.g., unemployment insurance and industrial accident insurance); (6) a decline in prounion attitudes among workers; and (7) increased employer resistance to unionization efforts.

In another contribution to this symposium, Richard Freeman (1988) also lists antiunion government policies—such as the actions of Ronald Reagan's administration in destroying the union representing US air controllers in response to their strike in 1981—as among the possible causes of deunionization. He concludes that the main reason for the decline in US private-sector unionization is increased management opposition to union organization, motivated by such profit-related factors as a rise in the union wage premium, increased foreign competition, and government deregulation policies. Still another factor frequently mentioned in recent years as contributing to the weakening of labor unions is the unskilled labor-displacing nature of new technology, including outsourcing.

There is, however, no general agreement among labor specialists concerning the relative importance of these various possible explanations. Initial research into the decline in union membership in the late 1970s and early 1980s (e.g., Dickens and Leonard 1985) stresses the importance of shifts in the composition of the labor force and the structure of production. Later studies de-emphasize this explanation, however, in part because these changes are themselves outcomes to be explained at a more fundamental level. Henry Farber and Alan Krueger (1992) conclude on the basis of survey data that virtually all of the decline in union membership from the 1970s to early 1990s was due to a decline in worker demand for union representation and that there was almost no change in the relative supply of union jobs. Of course, many of the same basic economic forces affecting employers' profit-oriented decisions could also affect workers' decisions about the desirability of union representation.

US union leaders themselves place much of the blame for deunionization on the actions of American corporations. In their view, corporate America's aggressive efforts to increase profits have led to a variety of business actions and public policies designed to reduce labor costs by weakening unions' bargaining power. These corporate actions range from efforts aimed at preventing domestic unionization and at decertifying existing union representation to importing intermediate inputs rather than producing them domestically and establishing (or threatening to establish) their own outsourcing facilities in lower-wage countries. With respect to governmental policies, union leaders maintain that corporate America has used its greater political funding and lobbying capabilities to secure both domestic legislation weakening the right of workers to organize and international legislation reducing the bargaining power of organized labor by promoting agreements with other countries that expand trade and foreign direct investment without ensuring the enforcement of core labor rights internationally.

The present study first describes the nature of the deunionization process during two decades, 1977–87 and 1987–97, both nationally and regionally. Then it focuses on one of the several suggested explanations for deunionization, namely, the increased openness of the United States to international trade. Utilizing microeconomic data collected as part of the US government's annual Sample Census of Population, I investigate statistically whether the increased openness of the United States to international trade during these years affected the employment of union workers disproportionately compared with nonunion workers, that is, more adversely (or less beneficially) than would be expected from the relative importance for overall employment of these two groups of workers. If so, is it a major possible explanatory factor for deunionization?

Chapter 2 summarizes the main features of the changes in the extent of national unionization rates between 1977–87 and 1987–97 among major industry groups and among workers with different levels of education. The chapter also examines and compares shifts during these periods in the proportion of unionized workers in manufacturing in each of nine US geographical regions. Finally, changes over time in the gap between the earnings of union versus nonunion workers are reported for all workers, as well as for workers divided into broad industrial sectors and levels of education.

Chapter 3 further describes the nature of the US deunionization process by investigating the extent to which the decline in the national unionization rate can be attributed to a broad decline in unionization rates within industries versus simply a shift in national employment shares among industries from those with high unionization rates to industries with low rates of unionization.[3] This analysis provides information on the extent to which deunionization is due to changes in the structure of industry employment associated with such factors as uneven technological change among industries and shifts in the industry pattern of spending by domestic and foreign consumers versus some general economic force such as a basic unfavorable change in the attitude and behavior of firms, workers,

---

3. Because the national unionization rate is a weighted average of the unionization rates of every industry (where the weights are industry employment shares of all union and nonunion workers nationally), the change in the national unionization rate during a particular period can be algebraically decomposed into that part attributable to redistribution of employment shares across industries (the weights) and that part due to changes in the percentage of workers unionized within the various industries.

and the government toward unions that reduces unionization rates within most industries. This analysis is undertaken both at the national level and also separately for each of the nine US regions. A final application of this decomposition technique examines the relative importance for the national rate of unionization of changes in each region's share of national employment versus declines in unionization within each region.

As background for the study's main empirical analysis in chapter 5, chapter 4 presents a brief analytical review of the likely ways in which not only increased international trade and foreign direct investment but also other major economic forces affected the US economy during the 1977–97 period. These forces include technological progress that resulted in a demand for relatively fewer less-skilled workers, taste shifts toward the greater consumption of services relative to manufactured goods, and increases in the supply of more-educated compared with basically educated workers that influenced the earnings levels and employment distribution of union and nonunion workers across industries.

Chapter 5 then investigates by means of regression analysis the relationship between industry changes both in imports and exports and in the employment of union workers and nonunion workers, taking into account industry changes in domestic spending (demand forces) and in labor-input requirements (technology forces). Attention is devoted not only to the relationship between changes in trade and changes in the total number of union and nonunion workers across industries but also to changes in the employment of union and nonunion workers who were basically educated (defined here as those with 12 or fewer years of formal education) versus those who were more-educated (here, those with 13 or more years of schooling). The industries covered in the regression analysis include services as well as manufacturing and primary-product sectors.

Chapter 6 concludes by summarizing the study's main findings. It also briefly discusses the need for more extensive adjustment assistance programs to deal better with the unemployment and earnings-loss problems often associated with deunionization.

To preview some of the main findings: only about one-quarter of the total decline in the national rate of unionization between 1977 and 1987 and just one-tenth of the total decline in the 1987–97 period can be attributed to between-industries shifts in national employment shares from more unionized to less unionized industries, holding constant the within-industries unionization rates of all industries. Thus, declines in rates of unionization within industries, holding industry national employment shares constant, respectively explain (in an accounting sense) three-quarters and nine-tenths of the national deunionization during the first and second decades. Separating the changes in the national unionization rate in the manufacturing sector alone into these two components indicates an even greater role for the within-industries effect in accounting for deunionization during the two periods.

Between-industries shifts in shares of national manufacturing employment account for only 11 percent of the decrease in the unionization rate in manufacturing during the 1977–87 decade, compared with 89 percent due to within-industries changes in manufacturing unionization rates. During the 1987–97 period, between-industries shifts in manufacturing had the effect of increasing the rate of unionization. Moreover, gains in national employment shares by the US southern and western regions served to reduce their overall unionization declines.

Although the significant change in imports and exports across almost all industries in both periods is a possible explanatory factor for the general decline in industry unionization rates, regression analysis indicates that increased international trade has not been the major factor in the decline. Factors other than changes in trade or in the other independent variables in the regressions (these other independent variables are changes in domestic spending on domestically produced goods and changes in labor requirements per unit of output) that are captured in the regression equation's constant term account for most of the deunionization. An antiunion shift in attitudes by most employers and workers across the economy, together with unfavorable new legislation and the hostile administration by government of existing labor laws—factors cited by labor unions and many labor economists as the main reason for deunionization—would be the type of "other factors" picked up by the constant term.

Trade has played a role in the deunionization process among basically educated union workers, in manufacturing, however. For the 1977–87 decade, for example, I estimate the disproportionately adverse (in terms of the relative importance of these two groups in the labor force) employment impact of increases in imports of manufactured goods on basically educated union compared with basically educated nonunion workers to be equal to about one-quarter of the negative impact on union membership that is measured by the constant term in the regression equation. In the 1987–97 decade, the employment-displacement pressures of increased imports were actually disproportionately lower on basically educated union workers than on basically educated nonunion workers.

However, increases in exports in the manufacturing sector during the 1987–97 period were unexpectedly associated with decreases (rather than increases) in the employment of basically educated union workers. I suggest that this effect, which almost offsets the favorable manner in which basically educated union workers fared on the import side, may be due to the positive correlation of export increases with such other factors as increases in foreign direct investment and foreign outsourcing. The main conclusion, however, is that factors other than industry changes in international trade or the other independent variables in the regression equation account for most of the decline in unionization in both periods.

2

Trends in National and Regional Unionization Rates and in Union Versus Nonunion Wages

National Trends in Unionization

Tables 2.1 and 2.2 indicate the key national trends in union membership between 1977 and 1997. As table 2.1 shows, the proportion of all workers who were union members fell sharply, from 25.0 percent in 1977 to 13.8 percent by 1997, with two-thirds of this decline taking place in the 1977–87 decade. The proportion of unionized workers fell in all three major industry groupings: primary products and construction, manufacturing, and the services sectors.[1] A further indication of the pervasiveness of the decline across the 137 industries in the data set is that the rate of unionization declined in all 7 primary-product and construction sectors between 1977 and 1997, in 73 of the 74 manufacturing sectors, and in all but 10 of the 56 services sectors. Among the three broad sectoral groups, manufacturing was the most heavily unionized throughout the period, followed by primary industries and construction and by the services sectors. However, unionization declined the most in relative terms in manufacturing, falling by more than half, from 38.0 percent in 1977 to 17.6 percent in 1997. Consequently, by 1997 the proportion of unionized workers in manufacturing was little more than 1 percentage point higher than in primary products plus construction, with services not far behind.

An important exception to the downward trend in unionization occurred in the public sector of the US economy. Among the 8.6 million

---

1. In absolute terms, union membership fell by 2.7 million between 1977 and 1987 and by 1.2 million between 1987 and 1997.

Table 2.1 Proportion of unionized workers by product sector and educational level, 1977–97 (percent)

Sector and education	1977	1987	1997
All unionized workers			
All sectors	25.0	17.5	13.8
Manufacturing	38.0	24.8	17.6
Services sectors	20.2	15.6	12.7
Primary industries and construction	26.9	18.3	16.3
Unionized workers with 12 or fewer years of education			
All sectors	28.5	19.3	14.3
Manufacturing	42.9	29.9	21.2
Services sectors	22.2	15.9	12.2
Primary industries and construction	28.1	19.1	15.1
Unionized workers with 13 or more years of education			
All sectors	18.6	15.3	13.4
Manufacturing	22.8	15.3	12.9
Services sectors	17.3	15.3	13.1
Primary industries and construction	22.9	16.2	18.7
All unionized workers in selected sectors			
1997 net importing sectors	33.0	20.1	13.8
1997 net exporting sectors	22.8	15.0	11.9
Apparel and accessories (except knits)	27.6	20.5	10.1
Blast furnaces, steelworks, rolling and finishing mills	77.4	56.7	46.2
Computers and related equipment	6.7	3.2	2.2
Eating and drinking places	8.6	3.1	2.4
Public administration	33.3	39.1	36.9

Source: Author's calculations.

individuals employed in public administration in 1997, for example, the unionization rate was 36.9 percent, as compared with 33.3 percent in 1977. In addition, unionization in such public-service areas as elementary and secondary schools and the US Postal Service remained steady during the period, at about 48 and 82 percent, respectively. (The unionization rates for these two sectors are not reported separately in table 2.1.) However, the share of unionized workers in most private-sector service areas fell sharply. The unionized proportion in eating and drinking places fell from 8.6 percent in 1977 to only 2.4 percent in 1997, for example.[2]

---

2. Labor economists, e.g., Freeman (1988), attribute the rise in unionization in the public sector to such factors as reduced management opposition owing to the passage of comprehensive collective bargaining laws and vote-seeking behavior by politicians.

Table 2.2 Distribution of unionized workers across product sectors and educational levels, 1977–97 (percent)

Sector and education	1977	1987	1997
Unionized workers			
Primary products and construction	12.1	11.1	11.2
Manufacturing	34.9	25.2	20.0
Services	53.0	63.7	68.8
Unionized workers			
With 12 or fewer years of education	73.8	60.1	48.0
With 13 or more years of education	26.2	39.9	52.0
Unionized workers with 12 or fewer years of education			
Primary products and construction	13.3	13.9	14.4
Manufacturing	40.3	32.9	28.2
Services	46.4	53.2	57.4
Unionized workers with 13 or more years of education			
Primary products and construction	9.0	6.7	8.2
Manufacturing	19.6	13.7	12.3
Services	71.4	79.6	79.5

Source: Author's calculations.

Not only were variations in unionization rates significant among broad groups of industries in the 1970s, but differences in unionization rates between basically educated and more-educated workers—that is, unionized workers with 12 or fewer years of education (i.e., basically educated) and unionized workers with 13 or more years of education (i.e., more-educated), respectively—were also large in this period. Whereas 28.5 percent of the first group were union members in 1977, only 18.6 percent of the more-educated group were unionized in that year. As in the case of differences in unionization rates among broad industrial categories, this difference between workers with different levels of schooling narrowed considerably by 1997, with the unionization share of basically educated workers falling to 14.3 percent and the proportion of more-educated union members declining only to 13.4 percent.[3] Because of the rapid rise in the number of more-educated workers over the period and the sharp fall in the number of basically educated workers, by 1997 the number of more-educated unionized workers exceeded the number of basically educated ones by 0.6 million.

---

3. The number of unionized workers with 12 or fewer years of education declined during the entire period by 7.1 million, or by 48 percent. In contrast, the number of unionized workers with 13 or more years of education rose during the period by 3.1 million, or by 59 percent.

Table 2.1 also indicates rates of unionization between 1977 and 1997 in the goods and services industries that in 1997 were either net importing or net exporting sectors. As the table shows, the 1977 unionization rate of 33.0 percent for net importing industries was more than 10 percentage points higher than in net exporting industries in 1977. The rate of unionization fell significantly in both categories between 1977 and 1997, though slightly more in the net importing sectors.[4]

Table 2.2 shows the distribution of union workers across product groups and by levels of education. It indicates, for example, that in 1997 only 20.0 percent of all union workers were employed in manufacturing activities, compared with 34.9 percent in 1977. The proportion of all union workers employed in the service sectors rose from 53.0 percent in 1977 to 68.8 percent in 1997. Another important relationship brought out in table 2.2 is the rapid rise in the proportion of more-educated union workers. In 1997, 52.0 percent of unionized workers had received 13 or more years of education, compared with only 26.2 percent in 1977. As the other two parts of the table also make clear, the share of basically educated workers employed in manufacturing was greater than the share of more-educated workers. The reverse was the case for the services industries.

Regional Trends in Unionization

Not only did the rate of unionization in manufacturing fall significantly for the country as a whole between 1977 and 1997, but it also fell sharply within each region of the country, as table 2.3 indicates.[5] Unionization in the manufacturing sector decreased between these years by 50 percent or more in seven of the nine regional groups of states and by more than 60 percent in the two far western regions. The extent of unionization also varies widely among regions, as it does among industries. In 1977, the proportion of unionized workers in the most unionized region, the Upper Midwest (region 5), was almost two and a half times as large as in the least unionized region, the South (region 4), and the ratio was even larger in 1997.

Trends in the Earnings of Union
Relative to Nonunion Workers

Given the dramatic decline in the rate of US unionization in the last quarter of the 20th century, the behavior of the wages of union versus

---

4. The unionization rate in those industries in which there was no trade at all in 1997 was 14 percent.

5. It was not always possible to follow conventional regional breakdowns owing to the need to obtain an adequate sample size of union workers for each region.

Table 2.3 Proportion of unionized workers in manufacturing by region and year, 1977–97 (percent)

Region	1977	1987	1997
1. New England	29.2	18.2	12.4
2. New York and New Jersey	44.8	27.9	22.5
3. Pennsylvania, Delaware, Maryland, Virginia, and West Virginia	47.5	30.7	21.8
4. North Carolina, South Carolina, Georgia, Florida, Alabama, Mississippi, Tennessee, and Kentucky	21.2	13.0	9.5
5. Ohio, Indiana, Illinois, Michigan, Wisconsin, and Minnesota	52.0	35.7	25.7
6. Louisiana, Texas, Arkansas, Oklahoma, and New Mexico	27.6	17.9	12.3
7. Missouri, Iowa, Nebraska, Kansas, North Dakota, South Dakota, Montana, Wyoming, Utah, and Colorado	34.9	21.7	17.1
8. California, Nevada, Arizona, and Hawaii	30.7	18.2	10.5
9. Oregon, Washington, Idaho, and Alaska	46.7	29.2	18.6

Source: Author's calculations.

nonunion workers during the period is of particular interest. Table 2.4 presents information on this issue. It shows, first, that unionized workers earn considerably more than do nonunion workers. Average real weekly earnings for union workers fell slightly between 1977 and 1997, however, whereas the earnings of nonunion workers rose somewhat. This means that the union/nonunion earnings ratio of 1.40 (a 40 percent wage premium for union workers) for all workers in 1977 fell modestly to 1.32 by 1997.[6] For workers in the manufacturing sector, the union wage premium was considerably lower than for all workers: only 19 percent in 1977 and 16 percent in 1997. The greatest earnings gap among the three broad industry groups is in primary products and construction, followed by the services sectors.[7]

Table 2.4 also provides information on the premium earned by union versus nonunion workers for basically educated ones compared with those educated beyond the high school level. One difference between the two groups that stands out for the all-sectors category is the considerably higher ratio of weekly earnings of union members relative to nonunion

6. Each industry's earnings ratio for a particular group of workers is weighted by the employment of that group in the industry.

7. The high ratio in the primary-production and construction group is due to the high union wage premium in mining, in oil and gas extraction, and in the construction sector.

Table 2.4 Earning levels and ratios of union and nonunion workers by sector and educational level, 1977–97

Levels or ratios	1977	1987	1997
Weekly earnings (1983 dollars)			
Union workers	552.69	556.45	546.96
Nonunion workers	393.76	402.62	413.86
Union/nonunion earnings ratio			
All sectors	1.40	1.38	1.32
Manufacturing	1.19	1.14	1.16
Services sectors	1.40	1.40	1.31
Primary industries and construction	1.87	1.72	1.69
Union/nonunion earnings ratio for workers with 12 or fewer years of education			
All sectors	1.58	1.60	1.51
Manufacturing	1.34	1.36	1.38
Services sectors	1.59	1.59	1.45
Primary industries and construction	1.97	1.92	1.80
Union/nonunion earnings ratio for workers with 13 or more years of education			
All sectors	1.18	1.18	1.19
Manufacturing	0.92	0.93	0.99
Services sectors	1.19	1.21	1.20
Primary industries and construction	1.55	1.45	1.39
Union/nonunion earnings ratio in selected sectors			
1997 net importing sectors in manufacturing	1.21	1.16	1.18
1997 net exporting sectors in manufacturing	1.14	1.11	1.12
Union 1997 net exporting/union 1997 net importing	1.07	1.08	1.04
Nonunion 1997 net exporting/nonunion 1997 net importing	1.14	1.13	1.12

Source: Author's calculations.

workers among basically educated individuals than among more-educated ones. The all-sectors ratio for each of these education groups is comparatively stable over time, however, with the union earnings premium for basically educated workers falling from 58 percent in 1977 to 51 percent in 1997 and the premium for more-educated workers actually rising from 18 percent to 19 percent. The rank order of the ratios among broad industry groups for both education groups is the same as for all workers combined.

The level and change over time in the union/nonunion earnings ratio in the manufacturing sector are of particular interest. Although the earnings of basically educated union workers in this sector were more than 30 percent higher than the earnings of basically educated nonunion workers throughout the period, more-educated union workers in manufacturing actually earned slightly less than more-educated nonunion workers. The importance of the shift in the composition of the workforce toward more-educated workers in affecting the union/nonunion earnings ratio for all workers is also brought out clearly in the manufacturing sector. The union/nonunion earnings ratio in manufacturing rose somewhat for both the basically educated and more-educated groups separately, whereas this ratio actually fell slightly between 1977 and 1997 for the two groups combined.

Such an outcome is possible because the ratio for both groups is a weighted average of the ratios for the two education groups separately, where the weights are the proportions of workers in each education group. The increased weight given to the more-educated group in 1997 than in 1977 (55.0 percent compared with 37.1 percent), coupled with the much lower union/nonunion earnings ratio for the more-educated groups, caused the ratio for both groups combined to decline between these years.[8]

A final set of statistics in table 2.4 relates to the earnings of union versus nonunion workers in net importing and net exporting industries. Industries are first divided into those with a net import surplus in 1997 and those with a net export surplus in that year. The ratio of union to nonunion earnings is calculated not only for these industries in 1997 but also for the same industries in 1987 and 1977.

As the numbers indicate, union workers earn a premium over nonunion workers in both the net exporting and net importing industries during the entire period; but this premium declined between 1977 and 1997. However, throughout this period, the earnings ratio of union to nonunion workers remained higher in net importing manufacturing industries than in net exporting manufacturing sectors. Another relationship confirmed in table 2.4 is that both union and nonunion workers earned more in net exporting than in net importing sectors (see the bottom two rows).

---

8. Regressing relative industry changes in the ratio of average weekly wages of union members to nonunion employees on relative industry changes in shipments, imports, exports, and the industry level of the ratio at the beginning of each period yields a statistically negative coefficient for the initial level of the ratio but insignificant coefficients for the other variables.

3

Changes in Unionization Rates:
A Decomposition Analysis

This chapter reports fairly standard algebraic techniques for decomposing changes in unionization rates into two parts. The first, generally termed the "between-industries" (or "between-regions") component, measures the part of the total decrease in the unionization rate attributable to decreases in the share of unionized workers employed in more unionized compared with less unionized industries (or regions), holding unionization rates within each industry (or region) constant.

The second component, the "within-industries" (or "within-regions") effect, measures the part of the decline in the unionization rate associated with decreases in rates of unionization within the industries (or regions), holding the shares of unionized workers employed in each industry (or region) constant. A finding that the decline in the share of workers who are unionized is associated mainly with changes in the percentage distribution of union workers across industries or regions (the between-industries or -regions component) would tend to rule out an economywide unfavorable shift in the attitude of most employers and employees toward unions or an unfavorable change in government policies toward unions as being the key factors accounting for deunionization. Instead, such factors as uneven technological change among industries (or regions) and shifts in the pattern of spending across industries (or regions) by domestic and foreign consumers would more likely be the main causes of deunionization.

Industry Effects on the National Rate of Unionization

The national share of workers who are unionized can be usefully expressed as the sum across all industries of the share of workers in each industry who are unionized multiplied by each industry's share of all employed workers. Letting U_i be the number of unionized workers in any industry i (where the number of industries runs from $i = 1$ to $i = n$), ΣU_i be the sum of unionized workers (U_i) across all i industries, L_i be the total number of workers (unionized plus nonunionized) in industry i, and ΣL_i be the sum of union plus nonunion workers across all industries, this can be expressed as the equation

$$\Sigma U_i / \Sigma L_i = \Sigma(U_i / L_i * L_i / \Sigma L_i) \tag{3.1}$$

Denoting U_i / L_i as u_i and $L_i / \Sigma L_i$ as l_i, this can, in turn, be expressed more simply as

$$\Sigma s_i = \Sigma(u_i l_i) \tag{3.2}$$

where Σs_i is the sum across industries of each industry's fraction of unionized workers to all union plus nonunionized workers in the economy (the national unionization rate) and $\Sigma(u_i l_i)$ is the sum across all industries of each industry's unionization rate multiplied by its employment share of the national labor force.

Expressing the national unionization rate in this manner brings out clearly that this rate is affected both by the relative importance of the industry's workers (unionized plus nonunionized) in the national labor force and by each industry's own unionization rate. Changes over time in each industry's ratio of unionized workers to all workers rate can be approximated as

$$\Delta s_i = \Delta u_i l_i + \Delta l_i u_i \tag{3.3}$$
{Within-   {Between-
industries   industries
component}   component}

where $\Delta u_i l_i$ measures the effect of a change in industry i's own unionization rate on Δs_i, holding its share of the labor force constant (this is termed the within-industries component of the change in the left-hand-side variable) and $\Delta u_i l_i$ measures the effect of a change in the proportion of all workers employed in industry i (Δl_i) on the change in the industry's ratio of union workers to all workers in the economy (Δs_i), holding the unionization rate in the industry (u_i) constant (this is generally called the between-industries component of the change in the left-hand-side variable). Summing these terms over all industries yields the estimated national change in the proportion of all workers who are unionized.

Richard Freeman (1988) reports that studies of the 1960s through 1970 involving statistical exercises decomposing the change in the national unionization rate into these two components attribute 50–70 percent of the decline in private-sector unionization to the between-industries component, whereas analyses for the mid-1970s to mid-1980s find that less than half of the unionization decline can be assigned to this factor (Dickens and Leonard 1985). Henry Farber and Alan Krueger (1992) conclude from an analysis of the 1977–91 period[1] that only about 25 percent of the overall decline in the unionization rate can be accounted for by the between-industries component.[2]

Table 3.1 shows the results of the decomposition exercise during the 1977–87 and 1987–97 periods for the 137 industries included in the database.[3] As is indicated in the first column of the table, out of the –7.5-percentage-point change (a 30 percent decrease) in the unionization rate for all industries during the 1977–87 decade, 5.5 percentage points (about 73 percent of the total decline) is attributable to within-industries decreases in unionization rates, whereas 2.0 percentage points (about 27 percent of the decline) are due to changes in industry shares of total employment away from more highly unionized industries and toward less unionized industries. In the 1987–97 period, not only was the 3.7-percentage-point decline in the national unionization rate less than in the earlier decade, but between-industries shifts in union employment contributed only 11.1 percent to the overall percentage-point decline in the national unionization rate.

---

1. Farber and Krueger use regression analysis to determine the relative importance of structural changes in accounting for the total change in unionization and also include a broader set of structural variables.

2. Three points are especially important to stress with regard to this kind of standard decomposition analysis. The first is that it is purely an accounting exercise. Any economic implications drawn from the results must be based on prior theoretical reasoning concerning the nature of the underlying causes of changes in the variables.

The second point to emphasize is that the results are quite sensitive to the number of industries included in the analysis. For example, if the whole economy is treated as a single industry, all of the change in the national unionization rate would be attributable to the within-industries component, because the proportion of all workers employed in the single industry would always be 1 and therefore Δl_i would be zero. The third point is that there are a number of different ways of decomposing changes into between-industries and within-industries components. An important difference is whether one uses the initial values of the variables, e.g., their values in an earlier year, and the changes in these variables to their subsequent values, e.g., a latter year, or whether one begins with the end-period values and uses the changes in these values to their earlier levels.

There is no mathematical or economic reason why one approach should be preferred to the other, and yet—unless the changes are very small—the relative magnitudes of the two components can vary appreciably. The approach followed here is to undertake the decomposition in both ways and report the average of the two methods in order to minimize the bias associated with each method.

3. See appendix B for the list of industries.

Table 3.1 Estimated changes in unionization rates due to within-industries shifts in unionization rates and between-industries shifts in employment, 1977–87 and 1987–97 (percentage-point change and percent share)

Contribution	All industries Point change	Share	Primary products Point change	Share	Manufacturing Point change	Share	Services Point change	Share
1977–87								
Total change[a]	−7.5	100	−8.6	100	−13.2	100	−4.6	100
Within-industries contribution[b]	−5.5	73.3	−10.0	114.9	−11.7	88.5	−3.0	65.2
Between-industries contribution[c]	−2.0	26.7	1.3	−14.9	−1.5	11.4	−1.6	34.8
1987–97								
Total change[a]	−3.7	100	−2.0	100	−7.2	100	−2.9	100
Within-industries contribution[b]	−3.2	89.9	−2.2	104.8	−7.4	104.2	−2.4	85.7
Between-industries contribution[c]	−0.4	11.1	0.1	−4.8	0.3	−4.2	−0.4	14.3

a. Because of rounding, the sums of the within-industries and between-industries percentage-point changes, on which the percent shares are based, may not add up exactly to the total percentage-point changes, which are calculated from table 2.1.
b. The effect, summed across all the industries making up an industry group, of a change in an industry's own unionization rate on the change in the industry's proportion of union workers to all workers in the industry group, holding the industry's share of all the workers in the industry constant.
c. The effect, summed across all the industries making up an industry group, of a change in an industry's share of all workers in the industry group on the change in the industry's proportion of union workers in the industry group, holding the industry's unionization rate constant.

Source: Author's calculations.

The next three pairs of columns in table 3.1 show this breakdown for broad groups of industries. Interestingly, changes in the distribution of industry employment (the between-industries component) in the primary-products and construction group (7 industries) had a positive effect on the overall unionization rate in both periods, largely because the two main gainers in employment shares, landscape and horticultural services and construction, were more highly unionized than the main market-share loser, agricultural products. The between-industries component was negative for both the manufacturing (74 industries) and the services group (56 industries) between 1977 and 1987, accounting for about 11 percent of the decline in the share of unionized workers in manufacturing and about 35 percent of the overall decline in services, as more highly unionized sectors lost employment shares to less-unionized industries. The decomposition results for the following decade indicate that the significant decline in deunionization attributable to within-industries declines in unionization rates held for all three sectors. Between-industries employment shifts in the primary-product and manufacturing sectors had the effect during the 1987–97 period of increasing the overall unionization rate in these sectors, but for services the between-industries component was negative.

The main conclusion to be drawn from table 3.1 is that, consistent with the more recent studies of labor economists, the declines in the rate of unionization in the US economy as a whole and in broad subgroupings of industries are mainly the result of decreases in unionization rates within industries rather than shifts in the distribution of employment from industries with high to low unionization rates. Moreover, the relative importance of between-industries employment shifts in bringing about deunionization seems to have decreased significantly. One implication of this finding is that broad antiunion attitudes and policies on the part of employers and the government cannot be ruled out as the major factor accounting for deunionization.[4]

Industry Effects on Regional Unionization Rates in Manufacturing

People often suspect that deunionization has been aggravated by shifts from the North to the South (and the West) in the United States, just as they also suspect the influence of declines in manufacturing employment. Table 3.2 presents the results of decomposing the changes in manufacturing unionization rates[5] (comparably detailed data for nonmanufacturing were not available) in each of nine regions in the United States analyzed

---

4. As is explained more fully in the next chapter, one can draw only limited conclusions about which factors are most important in accounting for deunionization, because most of the possible economic factors tend to affect both the between-industries and within-industries components.

5. The industry breakdown within the manufacturing sector consists of the 20 industries making up the Commerce Department's 2-digit 1987 Standard Industrial Classification (SIC) system: (1) food and kindred products; (2) tobacco products; (3) textile mill products; (4) apparel and other textile products; (5) lumber and wood products; (6) furniture and fixtures; (7) paper and allied products; (8) printing and publishing; (9) chemicals and allied products; (10) petroleum and coal products; (11) rubber and miscellaneous plastics; (12) leather and leather products; (13) stone, glass, and clay products; (14) primary metal industries; (15) fabricated metal products; (16) industrial machinery and equipment; (17) electronic and other electric equipment; (18) transportation equipment; (19) instruments and related products; and (20) miscellaneous manufacturing products. Unionization rates for the services sector are not available on a regional basis.

Table 3.2 Estimated percent distribution of changes in regional unionization rates in manufacturing due to within-industries and between-industries shifts in employment, 1977–87 and 1987–97 (percentage-point change and percent share)

Region[a]	1977–87			1987–97		
	Point change in unionization rate	Share due to within-industries component[b]	Share due to between-industries component[b]	Point change in unionization rate	Share due to within-industries component[b]	Share due to between-industries component[c]
1	-11.0	97.3	2.7	-5.8	93.0	7.0
2	-16.9	87.9	12.1	-5.4	102.9	-2.9
3	-16.8	84.6	15.4	-8.9	95.0	5.0
4	-8.2	106.9	-6.9	-3.5	116.2	-16.2
5	-16.3	94.5	5.5	-10.0	94.7	5.3
6	-9.7	100.5	-0.5	-5.6	93.9	6.1
7	-13.2	94.9	5.1	-4.6	90.7	9.3
8	-12.5	86.6	13.4	-7.7	94.7	5.3
9	-17.5	82.5	17.5	-10.6	84.6	15.4

a. Explanation of regional codes: 1: New England; 2: New York and New Jersey; 3: Pennsylvania, Delaware, Maryland, Virginia, and West Virginia; 4: North Carolina, South Carolina, Georgia, Florida, Alabama, Mississippi, Tennessee, and Kentucky; 5: Ohio, Indiana, Illinois, Michigan, Wisconsin, and Minnesota; 6: Louisiana, Texas, Arkansas, Oklahoma, and New Mexico; 7: Missouri, Iowa, Nebraska, Kansas, North Dakota, South Dakota, Montana, Wyoming, Utah, and Colorado; 8: California, Nevada, Arizona, and Hawaii; 9: Oregon, Washington, Idaho, and Alaska.

b. The effect, summed across all the industries making up an industry group, of a change in an industry's own unionization rate on the change in the industry's proportion of union workers to all workers in the industry group, holding the industry's share of all the workers in the industry constant.

c. The effect, summed across all the industries making up an industry group, of a change in an industry's share of all workers in the industry group on the change in the industry's proportion of union workers in the industry group, holding the industry's unionization rate constant.

Source: Author's calculations.

in table 3.2[6] into the part attributable to shifts in the structure of industry employment across each region (the between-industries component for each region) and the part attributable to decreases in industry unionization rates within each region (the within-industries component for each region).[7]

In other words, the decomposition undertaken for the economy as a whole reported in table 3.1 is undertaken for each region.[8] The effect of changes in a region's manufacturing structure, possibly due to shifts in production from or to other regions within the country, on a region's overall unionization rate has long been of interest. The first and fourth columns of table 3.2 indicate the percentage-point changes in the share of unionized workers in each of the nine regions between 1977 and 1987 and 1987 and 1997, respectively.

As in the case of the national data, table 3.2 indicates that between-industries changes in the distribution of employment among the 20 manufacturing industries have not been a major factor contributing to the overall decrease in unionization for any region; decreases in unionization rates within industries have been much more important. In the 1977–87 decade, the relatively largest adverse effects from shifts in industry employment structures occurred in the Mid-Atlantic area (regions 2 and 3) and the Pacific area (regions 8 and 9), but even the highest of these (region 9) was only 17.5 percent. In New York and New Jersey (region 2), the industry contributing the largest negative effect from between-industries changes in the first period was the apparel sector,[9] which both had a high share in the loss of employment and was highly unionized.[10]

---

6. It was not always possible to follow conventional regional breakdowns owing to the need to obtain an adequate sample size of union workers for each region.

7. For the sake of simplicity, the within-industries and between-industries components of the percentage-point changes in unionization for each region are reported only as percentage shares of the percentage-point changes rather than, as in table 3.1, in both percentage shares and percentage-point changes.

8. There is an equation similar to equation 3.3 in the text for each region, where the industry coverage is confined to the 20 manufacturing sectors listed in footnote 5 above.

9. The discussion here (and throughout this section) concerning the relative importance of particular industries toward contributing to the between-industries and within-industries components is based on detailed tables (not presented here, but available from the author) of the behavior of each of the 20 industries in each of the nine regions.

10. As is evident from the analysis of the between-industries and within-industries components on the change in the national unionization rate (see equation 3.3), the magnitude of an industry's between-industries effect on the change in a region's unionization rate depends on the change in the share of the region's workers employed in the industry and on the level of the industry's unionization rate. Similarly, the impact of an industry's within-industries effect on a region's unionization rate depends on the change in the industry's unionization rate and on the proportion of the region's workers employed in the industry.

In Pennsylvania, Delaware, Maryland, West Virginia, and Virginia (region 3) for the 1977–87 period, the largest between-industries contribution to the overall decline in unionization was made by the highly unionized primary metal industries, which suffered the largest employment-share loss. The largest positive between-industries effect (i.e., boosting unionization) in both regions 2 and 3 came from the printing and publishing industry. In regions 9 and 8 of the upper and lower Pacific area (Oregon, Washington, Alaska, and Idaho and California, Arizona, Nevada, and Hawaii), lumber and wood products and food and kindred products, respectively, were the largest contributors to the relatively high negative impact of between-industries changes in employment shares.

Region 4 (South) was the only area in which changes in the distribution of employment together with levels of industry unionization (the between-industries employment effect) had an appreciable positive impact on overall unionization rates in the 1977–87 period.[11] Employment shares in region 4 for textiles and apparel decreased appreciably, but the region's low unionization rates in these sectors mitigated the negative impact of this shift on the overall unionization rate. The positive effect of the region's diversification into more unionized industries—such as electric and electronic equipment, transportation equipment, and instruments and related products—more than offset the negative impact of the relative shift out of textiles and apparel.

The comparatively low adverse effect on overall unionization of between-industries employment shifts in region 5 (the Midwest) between 1977 and 1987 is somewhat surprising, because of the declines in employment shares of such highly unionized sectors as leather and leather products; stone, clay, and glass products; primary metal industries; and transportation equipment. However, relative shifts in employment toward such sectors as fabricated metal products and rubber and miscellaneous plastics, which are among the more-unionized sectors in the region, acted to moderate these adverse between-industries effects.

In the 1987–97 period, there was both a slowing of the pace of deunionization and a decline in the relative importance of the between-industries component in the overall change in unionization for the four regions where the relative importance of this component had been the highest (though modest) in the previous decade: regions 2, 3, 8, and 9. Not only did the between-industries employment component for the South (region 4) continue to have the effect of increasing unionization, as in the previous decade, but employment shifts in New York and New Jersey (region 2) also had this effect. Textiles and apparel continued to decline in region 4 as a source of employment, but continued structural diversi-

11. In region 6 (Texas, Oklahoma, Louisiana, Arkansas, and New Mexico) the between-industries effect contributed slightly to increasing the overall unionization rate.

fication in other manufacturing industries where the unionization rates were higher acted to produce a net positive between-industries effect.

The Pacific Northwest (region 9) again had the largest relative adverse between-industries employment effect, in which the continued sharp fall in the employment share of the fairly well unionized lumber and wood products sector played the most important role. Also again, the adverse structural employment effect within the Midwest (region 5) was relatively small.

Regional Effects on the National Unionization Rate in Manufacturing

A final decomposition exercise is reported in table 3.3. This focuses on the change on the national unionization rate in manufacturing due to within-regions shifts (rather than within-industries changes) in unionization rates for manufacturing and to between-regions shifts in the distribution of manufacturing employment (rather than, as in table 3.1, on between-industries changes). Such an analysis indicates the extent to which the national unionization rate for manufacturing is affected by a change in unionization rates within the different regions versus a redistribution of national employment among the regions from more unionized regions toward less unionized ones, or vice versa.

The procedure for dividing the change in the national unionization rate in manufacturing into these two components is the same as described by the three equations set forth in the first section of this chapter except that the subscript i now refers to a region rather than an industry and the industry group being analyzed is confined to manufacturing. Specifically, the national unionization rate in manufacturing is the sum of all the union workers in each region divided by the sum of all union and nonunion workers in each region, namely, $\Sigma U_i/\Sigma L_i$, where the regions run from $i = 1$ to $i = 9$. This national unionization rate can be expressed as the weighted average of the manufacturing unionization rates in each region, U_i/L_i, where the weights are each region's share of the national labor force, $L_i/\Sigma L_i$. Expressed as an equation,

$$\Sigma U_i/\Sigma L_i = U_1/L_1 * L_1/\Sigma L_i + U_2/L_2 * L_2/\Sigma L_i + \ldots + U_9/L_9 * L_9/\Sigma L_i \qquad (3.4)$$

Denoting U_i/L_i as u_i and $L_i/\Sigma L_i$ as l_i, the change in the national unionization rate in manufacturing during a time period can be approximated as

$$\Delta(\Sigma U_i/\Sigma L_i) = \Sigma(\Delta u_i l_i + \Delta l_i u_i) \qquad (3.5)$$

{Within-
regions
component}

{Between-
regions
component}

Table 3.3 Regional distribution of change in national unionization rate in manufacturing due to within-regions shifts in unionization rates and between-regions shifts in employment shares, 1977–87 and 1987–97 (percentage-point change)

Region[a]	1977–87 Point change in unionization rate	1977–87 Point change due to within-regions component[b]	1977–87 Point change due to between-regions component[c]	1987–97 Point change in unionization rate	1987–97 Point change due to within-regions component[b]	1987–97 Point change due to between-regions component[c]
1	-0.7	-0.7	0.0	-0.5	-0.3	-0.2
2	-2.2	-1.7	-0.5	-1.2	-0.5	-0.7
3	-2.3	-1.7	-0.6	-1.0	-0.8	-0.2
4	-0.9	-1.3	0.4	-0.5	-0.6	0.1
5	-5.2	-3.8	-1.4	-2.6	-2.1	-0.5
6	-0.5	-0.6	0.1	-0.2	-0.4	0.2
7	-0.6	-0.7	0.1	-0.1	-0.3	0.2
8	-0.4	-1.1	0.1	-1.0	-0.9	-0.1
9	-0.4	-0.5	0.1	-0.1	-0.3	0.2
Total change	-13.2	-12.1	-1.1	-7.2	-6.2	-1.0

a. Explanation of regional codes: 1: New England; 2: New York and New Jersey; 3: Pennsylvania, Delaware, Maryland, Virginia, and West Virginia; 4: North Carolina, South Carolina, Georgia, Florida, Alabama, Mississippi, Tennessee, and Kentucky; 5: Ohio, Indiana, Illinois, Michigan, Wisconsin, and Minnesota; 6: Louisiana, Texas, Arkansas, Oklahoma, and New Mexico; 7: Missouri, Iowa, Nebraska, Kansas, North Dakota, South Dakota, Montana, Wyoming, Utah, and Colorado; 8: California, Nevada, Arizona, and Hawaii; 9: Oregon, Washington, Idaho, and Alaska.

b. The percentage-point contribution of a region to the percentage-point change in the national unionization rate for manufactures of a change in the region's unionization rate, holding its share of the national labor force constant.

c. The percentage-point contribution of a region to the percentage-point change in the national unionization rate for manufactures of a change in the region's share of the national labor force, holding its unionization rate constant.

Source: Author's calculations.

where the terms are summed over the nine regions. The results shown in table 3.3 indicate that only a small part of the decline in the overall unionization rate in manufacturing is attributable to a relative shift of the workforce from more-unionized to less-unionized regions. The South and all regions west of the Mississippi gained in national employment shares in the 1977–87 period and also in the following decade, with the exception of region 8. In contrast, the Midwest and all the northeastern regions lost in relative employment terms.

Because the unionization rate was higher in those regions that lost in employment-share terms than those that gained, the redistribution of the national labor force had the net effect of reducing the national unionization rate in manufacturing. The importance of this redistribution effect in accounting for the overall deunionization in manufacturing unionization rate was modest, however, compared with the effect of the declines in unionization rates within all regions. For example, of the 13.2-percentage-point decline in the national unionization rate in manufacturing between 1977 and 1987[12] (see the bottom row of table 3.3), 12.1 points (92 percent) is attributable to within-regions decreases in unionization rates and only 1.1 points (8 percent) to a redistribution of employment among the regions from more-unionized regions to less-unionized ones. As was pointed out above, the national unionization rate fell much less during the 1987–97 period, namely, only 7.2 percentage points, but the 1.0-percentage-point decline attributable to between-regions shifts in employment amounts to 14 percent of the total percentage-point decline.

Although every region contributed to the national decline in the rate of unionization, the differences among regions in the extent and nature of this contribution varied widely. The Midwest (region 5) stands out in both periods as the most significant contributor to the overall decrease in unionization, both because it had the highest proportion of the nation's unionized manufacturing workers (26 percent in 1977) and it lost national employment share. New York and New Jersey (region 2) and Pennsylvania, Delaware, Maryland, Virginia, and West Virginia (region 3) were also important sources of the overall decline in unionization, especially in the 1977–87 period, as the regional distribution of manufacturing shifted in favor of the South and the West.

---

12. Because of rounding, the sums for the nine regions may not exactly equal the total change for the country.

4

The Effects of Trade and Other Economic Factors on the Rate of Unionization: An Analytical Review

The main empirical focus of this study is on the role of increased international trade in accounting for deunionization in the United States. To explain and then estimate that role empirically in chapter 5, it is also important to understand how other real-side (in contrast to monetary-side) economic forces influencing the US economy may have affected the rate of unionization.

Consequently, this chapter briefly reviews analytically the manner in which increased international trade and three other major real-side economic forces that influenced the US economy during the period of this study can affect the rate of unionization. Then chapter 5 statistically "explains" the effects of increases in trade on changes in unionized and nonunionized employment, taking account of the effects of changes in the other forces, and comparing their relative impact on deunionization. The four forces are

- the rapid expansion of international trade and foreign direct investment as new technologies have lowered transportation and communication costs internationally and permitted greater international fragmentation of production processes, as tariff and nontariff barriers to international commerce have been significantly reduced, and as various market-oriented reforms have been undertaken in many countries;

- the introduction of new technologies that have significantly raised gross domestic product but also have been biased toward the saving of less-skilled and less-educated labor;

- the continuing relative shift in consumer expenditures toward services and away from manufactured goods and primary products as US per capita income levels have risen; and

- the significant increase in the number of workers with more than a high school education relative to those with a high school education or less.

Increases in Trade and Foreign Direct Investment

Both union and nonunion workers are concerned about being displaced from their jobs because of increased imports and foreign outsourcing and, consequently, being forced to take lower-paying jobs or face downward wage pressures even if they do retain their jobs.[1] Union leaders are also concerned about the pressure that increased international competition can bring on employers to seek to deunionize their firms. In studying the economic effects of increased imports, economists have devoted most of their attention to the impact of lower-priced imports on the wages of workers in industrialized countries rather than on the redistribution of employment among industries in these countries brought about by increased imports.[2] For example, a large literature analyzes the extent to which greater imports have contributed to the widening wage gap between basically educated and more-educated workers since the late 1970s.[3]

Trade theory points out that there are several ways in which the distribution of workers across industries and trade can interact with each other. Consider a situation about which US labor leaders are very concerned, namely, the greater difficulty of increasing or even maintaining unionization rates in the manufacturing sector, which is the most highly unionized broad sector of the economy. Union leaders believe that unionization rates in manufacturing are falling owing to rising imports of less-skill-intensive manufactured goods from developing and transitional economies that are introducing modern technologies and institutions that enable them to better exploit their comparative advantage based on relatively large endowments of less-skilled labor. The net result is lower relative world prices for these manufactured goods and reductions in output and the number of union workers employed domestically in these industries.

If imports increase appreciably relative to exports in the manufacturing sector as a whole, general equilibrium effects within the economy

---

1. In his well-known study questioning whether globalization had gone too far, Rodrik (1997) stresses this point as a source of tension between the global market and social stability.

2. See Kletzer (2001) for a recent study that does deal with this latter issue.

3. See Cline (1997) and Slaughter (2000) for surveys of such analyses. Another recent study on the subject is Baldwin and Cain (2000).

are likely to bring about changes in relative factor prices as well as product prices.

For simplicity, consider an economy with only two factors of production, namely, basically educated and more-educated labor. Suppose the country is relatively abundant in more-educated labor and the technology of net import industries uses basically educated labor more intensively compared to more-educated labor than do net export industries.[4] The decline in the prices of imported goods relative to exported goods as imports increase will lead to not only a decline in output and employment in import-competing industries but a fall in the real wages of the productive factor used relatively intensively in producing imported goods, namely, basically educated labor. At the same time there will be a rise in the real wages of the factor used relatively intensively in producing export goods, namely, more-educated labor.[5]

The decline in the relative wages of basically educated labor also brings about the increased adoption of less-education-intensive production methods across all industries. Because unionization rates are higher in net importing manufacturing industries than in net exporting ones,[6] the shift of workers out of the former industries tends to reduce the rate of union membership in manufacturing.[7]

Another mechanism by which trade can affect domestic employment and unionization rates is the outsourcing by firms of their less skill-intensive domestic production activities to low-wage countries. This often involves establishing production affiliates abroad through direct foreign investment by these firms. Improvements in transportation and communications technology have acted to facilitate these activities. Not only does the foreign outsourcing tend to displace basically educated US workers, many of whom are unionized, but labor leaders also contend that threats by employers to shift production abroad are widely used to persuade their US workers to vote to deunionize. Of course, the alternative to not shifting less-skill-intensive processes abroad may be a complete closing down of the domestic industry.

---

4. The 1997 ratio of the number of workers in US manufacturing with 12 or fewer years of education to the number of workers in manufacturing with 13 or more years of schooling in net importing industries was 1.43, compared with a ratio of 1.04 in net exporting industries.

5. The relationship between product prices and factor prices (the Stolper-Samuelson theorem) is explained in detail in Deardorff and Stern (1994).

6. The 1997 ratio of union to nonunion workers in manufacturing industries with an import surplus was 0.22, compared with a ratio of 0.19 in net exporting manufacturing industries.

7. Union leaders are especially concerned that the displaced workers will be reemployed in nonunionized service sectors and that those remaining in the affected industries will agree to deunionize in an effort to preserve their jobs.

In many cases, foreign outsourcing involves exporting skill-intensive components of a product abroad and then continuing the processing of the final product by undertaking production activities that require less-skill-intensive labor on these components. If these less-skill-intensive activities complete the final stages of production, the completed product may then be exported to third countries; but if they do not, the assembled part of the final product may then be exported back to the home country for further high-skill processing activities. In either event, it is possible that increases in exports of skill-intensive components for further processing is associated with a decrease in the domestic employment of less-skilled workers formerly used in the production process.

Direct investment by foreign firms in the United States can also adversely affect unionization rates if these firms are more hostile toward unions and either place their production facilities in less unionized regions or resist unionization efforts more vigorously than do domestic firms.

Technological Changes

Consider the effects of a uniform improvement in technology in all domestic and foreign industries that is not biased toward either basically educated or more-educated labor—a change that raises the productivity of all productive factors in the same proportion. If preferences are also neutral—in the sense that consumers spend the same proportion of income on each good as their incomes rise—the net effect will be that the demand and supply curves for all products simply increase by a uniform proportion without any change in the relative prices of the products. Imports and exports will also rise by the same proportion, but there will be no changes in the utilization of basically educated and more-educated labor among industries. Real wages of these two types of labor will rise by the same proportion, but their wages relative to each other will remain unchanged.

In contrast, suppose that technical progress is uniform across domestic and foreign industries but economizes on basically educated labor and uses more-educated labor (so that firms utilize a lower proportion of basically educated relative to more-educated labor to produce a unit of output at prevailing wage rates for these two types of labor).

This type of technical change has the effect of increasing the output of products intensive in the use of basically educated workers relatively more than the output of products intensive in the use of more-educated workers at any given price ratio for the two product groups.[8] Because the United States imports goods and services that on balance more in-

---

8. This takes place as a consequence of the process of fully reemploying the displaced basically educated workers.

tensively use basically educated labor than do the products it exports, the relative prices of the goods intensive in the use of basically educated labor therefore tend to fall.

This relative price decline and the resulting decrease in the relative wages of basically educated labor tend to offset the increase in the output of less-education-intensive products compared with more-education-intensive ones. But such secondary effects usually are weaker than the primary effect. Thus, on balance, both basically educated and more-educated labor tend to shift out of more-education-intensive, export-oriented industries and into import-competing industries that intensively use basically educated labor. To the extent that this occurs, it should be easier to increase total union membership, because unionization rates are higher in the latter set of industries. Of course, if most new jobs are available only in the services sector or if labor-displacing technical progress is concentrated in the manufacturing sector, the overall rate of unionization could decline.

Relative Shifts in the Demand for Goods and Services

It is well known that as per capita income rises with product prices held fixed, the demand for services as a product group increases by a greater proportion than does the demand for primary products (e.g., agricultural goods) or for manufactured goods as a whole. This force acts to increase relative employment in the services sector. Not surprisingly—given the higher share of a product's value that is added directly by labor and capital in the average service industry than in the average manufacturing or primary-product industry, which relies more on intermediate inputs—the quantity of both basically educated and more-educated labor used per constant dollar's worth of services is greater than for manufactured or primary products.

Consequently, the service sector serves as an important employer of displaced or new supplies of basically educated and more-educated workers. Yet because the ratio of more-educated to basically educated labor used per constant dollar's worth of output is considerably greater in services than the other two product areas, a relative expansion of services tends to increase the wages of more-educated workers compared with those having a high school education or less.[9] Furthermore, because

9. In 1997, the ratios of more-educated workers to basically educated workers used per dollar of output were 1.08 for the service sector, 0.78 for manufacturing, and 0.48 for the primary-product and construction sectors. In 1977, the ratios were 0.70, 0.33, and 0.29, respectively. There are, of course, parts of the services sector, e.g., eating and drinking places, in which the ratio of the labor coefficients for more-educated workers to basically educated ones is lower than for manufacturing as a whole. In 1997, employment in the industries where this was the case amounted to 19 percent of all workers in the services sector.

the average rate of unionization is lower in services than in manufacturing or primary products and construction, the shift of workers into services tends to reduce the overall unionization rate.

Changes in the Relative Supply of Basically Educated Versus More-Educated Labor

Between 1977 and 1997, the number of workers with 13 or more years of education increased by about 120 percent—in contrast to a 5 percent increase in the number of workers with 12 or fewer years of schooling. This development changed the composition of the labor force so that more-educated surpassed basically educated workers by about 15 percent in 1997, whereas in 1977 the number of more-educated workers equaled only about 55 percent of the number of basically educated ones. This shift was, of course, not just accidental. The higher earnings of more-educated workers relative to basically educated ones—and especially the widening of this gap beginning in the late 1970s, brought about by the developments in trade, technology, and consumer preferences discussed above—stimulated increased investment in human capital.

A fundamental relationship of the standard trade model of many goods and many factors (but more goods than factors) is that if product prices remain unchanged, endowment changes tend on average to increase employment and output the most in those sectors making relatively intensive use of the factors that have increased the most in supply.[10] Because the United States is a significant supplier of goods in world markets, the increased supplies of goods intensively using the factors whose endowments have risen most will, however, likely decline somewhat in relative prices, along with the relative prices of their intensively used factors.

These effects tend to weaken the relationship that holds if product prices remain fixed. But as was noted in the discussion of technical change, such secondary effects usually do not completely offset primary effects. Thus, an increase in the supply of more-educated relative to basically educated individuals causes employment and output to increase the most in industries intensively using this type of labor and in which unionization rates are lower. It also tends to lower the wages of more-educated relative to basically educated labor.

---

10. The efforts of those factors increasing most in supply to become employed lead to short-run relative declines in the prices of these factors and thereby create new profit opportunities that bring about their employment, mainly in industries producing goods intensively utilizing these factors. With fixed product prices, this shift in the relative composition of output continues until the prices of all factors have returned to their initial equilibrium levels.

Another composition shift in the US labor force that may have contributed to deunionization is the rise in the proportion of foreign-born individuals from 5 percent in 1970 to 7.9 percent in 1990 and 10 percent in 2000 (US State Department; usinfo.state.gov/topical/global/immigration). Foreign-born workers, especially those who are among the basically educated members of the labor force, may be more responsive to the antiunion pressures brought by some employers. Although the proportion of foreign-born workers with a college education is the same as those born within the country, the proportion of foreign-born workers who have completed high school is considerable less than American-born workers: 67 versus 87 percent (US State Department data; as cited above).

Net Effects of the Four Economic Forces

Most of the major real-side economic forces discussed above are not favorable for the union movement in terms either of increasing union membership or raising the relative wages of members. Trade theory indicates that the increased relative importance of international trade in a country relatively abundant in highly educated labor (e.g., the United States), and where import-competing industries use basically educated labor more intensively on average than other industries, tends to lower the relative wages of basically educated workers and shift workers from import-competing industries into more competitive, export-oriented ones and into nontraded goods and services ones.

Because the bulk of US union members had received 12 or fewer years of education at the outset of the study and the unionization rate was (and has remained) lower in export-oriented and services industries than import-competing ones, the increased openness of trade tended to make it more difficult to increase the proportion of union members nationally. Increased US foreign direct investment and outsourcing abroad, as well as foreign direct investment in the United States, may also have contributed to the deunionization trend. Technological progress during the period operated to raise real gross domestic product, but its bias in displacing basically educated workers also had the effect of lowering their real wages compared with more-educated ones. However, the tendency for this type of technical change to shift workers into sectors intensively using basically educated labor operates in the direction of increasing the overall unionization rate.

The continuing shift in preferences away from primary products and manufactures and toward services tended to lower the overall unionization rate owing to the lower union membership rate in the service sectors as a group. Furthermore, because services tend on balance to use relatively more-educated labor, the relative wage pressure from this development operated in the early years of the study against most union members, who tended to be basically educated. Finally, the rapid growth in the supply of more-educated relative to basically educated workers tended to reduce the overall unionization rate, because the unionization rate among the first group of workers was considerably lower than among those with less schooling. However, in contrast to the increased openness to trade, the biased nature of technical change, and the relative shift in consumer spending toward services, this economic change tended to raise the wages of basically educated workers compared with more-educated ones.

We know, in fact, that the earnings of more-educated workers rose significantly relative to basically educated workers between 1977 and 1997. The ratio of the earnings of workers with 13 or more years of education to the earnings of workers with 12 or fewer years rose from 1.38 in 1977 to 1.52 by 1996.[11] Therefore, the relative wage effects of increased trade, education-biased technological progress, and increased relative demand for services must have dominated the opposite relative wage pressures coming from the increase in the relative supply of more educated workers.

Furthermore, even though more-educated workers became more costly relative to basically educated ones, the median industry labor requirement for more-educated labor increased from 2.9 workers per $1 million of output in 1977 to 3.2 in 1997, while the median industry labor requirement for basically educated labor decreased from 8.6 to 4.5 per $1 million of output.[12] This is evidence that technological progress meant relatively lower use of less-educated labor and higher use of more-educated labor. It also implies that increased import competition could not have played the dominant role in producing the widened wage gap between workers receiving schooling beyond high school and those with a high school education or less, because in that case the labor coefficient for the former group would have risen relative to that for less-educated workers.

Both output and employment increased to a greater extent in industries that relatively intensively used more-educated labor than in less-education-intensive industries. This implies that the distribution effects on output and employment of increased trade, of the shift in demand toward services, and of the increase in the supply of more-educated compared with basically educated workers dominated those of the biased (against basically educated workers) technical change.

---

11. See Baldwin and Cain (2000, figure 1 and table 1), for changes in this ratio between 1967 and 1996.

12. The median labor coefficient for more-educated and basically educated workers combined fell from 12.3 to 8.7 per $1 million of output between 1977 and 1997.

Consequently, the objectives of unions to increase the relative wages of their members and to increase the proportion of workers belonging to unions were hampered by real-side economic forces that brought about both a decline in the relative wages of that part of the labor force most unionized in 1977, namely, basically educated workers, and a relative shift in the industry distribution of the labor force toward sectors with lower rates of unionization, namely, more-education-intensive industries. The relative magnitude of such shifts and offsets is addressed in the next chapter.

5

Estimating the Impact of Increased Trade on the Employment of Union and Nonunion Workers

Statistical Model

Virtually all the fundamental forces described in chapter 4 have an impact on domestic output (i.e., shipments), on imports, and on exports (in constant dollars), and also on the number of union and nonunion workers employed. We have data on all these, and it is possible to utilize regression analysis to estimate quantitatively the average employment-shifting effects of industry changes in imports and exports (or any other of these variables) on changes in the employment of union versus nonunion workers (controlling for changes in the other variables) and thus to obtain estimates concerning whether trade changes in themselves are important factors associated with the changes in the number of union versus nonunion workers.

A useful way of proceeding is to begin with the identity that the number of workers employed domestically in the ith industry, L_i (where the number of industries goes from $i = 1$ to $i = n$), is equal to the industry's output, O_i, multiplied by the number of workers employed per unit value (in constant dollars) of the industry's output (the industry's labor coefficient, l_i). This can be expressed as the equation

$$L_i = O_i l_i \tag{5.1}$$

Changes in the number of workers in the industry over time, ΔL_i, can be approximated by totally differentiating equation 5.1:

$$\Delta L_i = \Delta O_i l_i + \Delta l_i O_i \tag{5.2}$$

Such economic forces as those discussed in the last chapter—increased trade, technological change, a greater consumption preference for services, and an increase in the supply of more educated workers relative to less educated workers—all affect both output and labor coefficients (and thus employment) across industries, with the observed changes in these variables being the net outcome of the interactions among these and other forces. To focus on the role of changes in trade on employment and to also control for the effects of changes in total domestic spending in an industry on the industry's imports, output, O_i, can be expressed as equal to domestic spending, A_i, on the output of the industry (either that which is produced by domestic or by foreign firms) minus imports, M_i, of an industry's products that are produced abroad plus exports, X_i, from the domestic industry. Thus, changes in L_i over time can be approximated as

$$\Delta L_i = l_i(\Delta A_i - \Delta M_i + \Delta X_i) + (A_i - M_i + X_i)\Delta l_i \qquad (5.3)$$

In our regression analysis based on equation 5.3, we take into account the well-established lack of perfect substitutability of imports and domestic counterparts measured in A_i. (This relationship is stressed in the so-called new trade theory.) Consequently, any change in fundamental transfer costs and tariffs that alters imports and their domestic counterparts (in A_i) will have effects on the L_i producing the A_i that depend on the degree of substitutability. We will let the data tell us how differences in both M_i and A_i affect L. We will not insist that each of them has the same effect (i.e., l_i), which we should if we really believed that imports and domestic goods in A_i were perfect substitutes.

The regression equation used to estimate the relationships between changes in industry imports and exports and changes in union and nonunion employment is the linear relationship

$$\Delta L_{iu} = \alpha + \beta_1 \Delta A_i + \beta_2 \Delta M_i + \beta_3 \Delta X_i + \beta_4 \Delta l_i + e_i \qquad (5.4)$$

where ΔL_{iu} is the change in the number of union workers employed in industry i during a particular time period (ΔL_{in} is the change in the number of nonunion workers employed in the industry during the same period) and the partial regression coefficients β_1, β_2, and β_3 indicate, respectively, the relationship between changes in domestic spending (ΔA_i), imports (ΔM_i), and exports (ΔX_i) on changes in union (or nonunion) employment (with different values for the βs being permitted), holding the other variables constant.

With regard to the fourth term, β_4, I am primarily interested in estimating the effect of changes in labor coefficients on the number of union and nonunion workers employed rather than in estimating how the changes in labor coefficients differed among the various components of domestic spending and spending by foreigners on domestic goods. Therefore, β_4 indicates the employment effect of a change in the industry's total labor coefficient (Δl_i) as influenced by such economic forces as technological change in the industry, changes in relative factor prices, and changes in relative factor supplies. I also introduce a constant term, α, into the regression equation to capture the effect on employment of omitted variables that are not closely associated with changes in the volume of international trade or in the equation's other independent variables. The last term in the equation, e_i, is assumed to be a well-behaved error term.[1]

Regressions are undertaken with not only changes in the number of all union and all nonunion workers employed as the dependent variables but also changes in the employment of union and nonunion workers who have either 12 or fewer years of education (i.e., basically educated workers) or 13 or more years of schooling (i.e., more-educated workers). In the latter instances, changes in the labor coefficients for basically educated or more-educated workers are used as the fourth independent variable to control for technological change in an industry.

Because regression equation 5.4 is based on equations 5.1 and 5.3, we expect positive partial regression coefficients for β_1, β_3, and β_4; that is, the greater the industry increases in domestic spending and exports during a time period, the greater the increases in industry union and nonunion employment, while the smaller the decreases in industry labor coefficients, the smaller the decreases in union and nonunion employment. A negative coefficient is expected for β_2; that is, the larger the increase in industry imports, the larger the expected negative adjustment-pressure impact on industry union and nonunion employment.

The question of prime interest is whether the negative adjustment impact of increases in imports and positive adjustment impact of increases in exports on union and nonunion employment are simply proportionate to the relative importance of union and nonunion workers in the

---

1. It should be noted that the outputs (shipments) of US industries and industry imports in the basic regression (equation 5.4) comprise both final goods and goods used as intermediate inputs in the production of the final goods. Thus, in the auto industry (1987 3-digit SIC industry 371), e.g., shipment values include the value of steering and suspension parts (1987 4-digit SIC 3714) as well as the final value of automobiles (1987 4-digit SIC 3711), which also includes the value of the steering and suspension parts.

If integrated firms producing autos make the steering and suspension parts themselves rather than purchasing them from other firms producing these parts and report to the Commerce Department only the value of their final product, autos, rather than also the production values of all the intermediate inputs for which the Commerce Department also collects information, the comparability of shipment values and industry labor coefficients over time would be affected simply by vertical integration in an industry, e.g., the purchase of the plant producing steering and suspension parts by the firm assembling the final automobiles. However, the Census Bureau asks firms to report separately the value of products that are transferred to other manufacturing plants for further product processing.

labor force or whether the decrease (or increase) in employment of union workers associated with increases in imports (or exports) is disproportionately greater (or less) than for nonunion workers. Furthermore, if trade does have disproportionate effects, how important is the trade factor in accounting for the decrease during the specific two periods in the number of union workers?

Data Issues

We utilize sample data on union and nonunion membership by industry (mainly at the 3-digit level of the US Commerce Department's Standard Industrial Classification, or SIC) and level of education from the US Census Bureau's Current Population Surveys. These data are supplemented with industry data on employment, shipments, and trade from the US Bureau of Labor Statistics, input-output tables prepared by the US Bureau of Economic Analysis, and the various economic censuses undertaken by the US Department of Commerce. The complete data set covers 137 industries composed of 74 manufacturing industries, 56 service industries, and 7 industries involving agriculture, mining, or construction during the two periods 1977–87 and 1987–97.[2]

Although a complete analysis of the relationships between trade and employment clearly requires the inclusion of industries producing services as well as goods, there are significant data problems concerning the reliability and uniformity of the coverage of international trade in services during the study period.[3] Unlike goods transactions, international service transactions usually generate no official records or customs documentation and involve many different forms of delivery. To compile statistics on international service transactions, the US government relies largely on periodic surveys of companies engaged in such activities. The difficulty of determining which firms and individuals are involved in cross-border trade in services and the relatively high costs of the surveys have resulted in the data on trade in services being much less complete and accurate than the data on trade in goods. Furthermore, the failure (largely for cost reasons) to revise earlier data, other than for a few years, after a new survey has been undertaken causes serious comparability problems over time with the data on international service transactions.

Unlike all the goods sectors, many service sectors in the data set list

---

2. See appendix A for a more detailed description of the data sources and appendix B for a complete list of the industries in the basic data set.

3. See Kester (1992, chap. 5) for a detailed description of the methods used to collect data on US services trade and discussions of the problems associated with these data.

trade only on the export side.[4] Yet because product differentiation exists within service sectors as well as within goods sectors, one expects "love-of-variety" preferences (discussed below) on the part of consumers to lead to two-way trade in service industries whenever transportation costs or other factors do not rule out trade completely. Recording only exports for many service sectors may be because of the greater difficulty in tracking imports of services or perhaps to political pressures to reduce the recorded size of the US trade deficit. I believe that the data are most reliable if both imports and exports are recorded in a particular service sector at the outset of a period. Therefore, the data set used for the regressions covering both goods and services includes only those service sectors in which trade is reported for both the import and export sides at the beginning and end of a period.

This procedure and the exclusion of sectors in which there are no recorded imports or exports reduce the number of industries included in the regressions covering both goods and services to 92 industries in the 1977–87 period (74 manufacturing, 12 services, and 6 primary-product industries) and 97 in the 1987–97 period (74 manufacturing, 17 services, and 6 primary-product industries).[5] However, as is further explained in discussing the regression results, questions still remain about the reliability of the data having this limitation on the nonmanufacturing industries included in the data set. Therefore, regressions are also undertaken on manufacturing industries alone, where the data seem more reliable. It is the results from this analysis of the manufacturing sector that are emphasized in the study.

Another issue that arises is whether to treat the employment effects of changes in an industry's trade on a net basis or to take independent account of both imports and exports in the same industry. One reason for such two-way trade is that product categories are often so broad (e.g., electrical machinery, electrical equipment, and electrical supplies) that some of the different products within a particular product class are used as intermediate inputs in producing other products within the same commodity classification. Consequently, output (including export) increases of the final goods are associated with import increases of the intermediate goods. Differences in home and foreign comparative-cost conditions among various goods within a product category also lead to both exports and imports within the same product group.

The "new" trade theory, which replaces the perfect-competition assumption of traditional trade theory with the assumption that markets

---

4. For the 1977–87 period, only export trade is reported in 55 percent of the 56 service sectors in the data set. No exports or imports are reported in another 23 percent of the service sectors.

5. As was mentioned above, the number of sectors in the complete database is 137.

are imperfectly competitive, provides additional explanations for the existence of two-way international trade—even within the very detailed product descriptions used by customs officials. One part of this theory assumes that imperfect competition arises because of differentiated products. Within particular well-defined product classifications (e.g., a refrigerator, a personal computer, or a restaurant meal), there are many varieties of the product that differ from each other for reasons other than price (e.g., color, speed versus memory, or style of cooking).

If individuals like to consume many varieties of a product (so-called love-of-variety behavior), the existence of both imports and exports within a specific product classification is easily explained. Residents of a country wish to purchase both home-produced and foreign-produced varieties of a particular product (e.g., a car made in the United States and a car made abroad), even if the varieties of the product do not differ in price. Thus, when the demand for a product increases because of a general increase in national income or a technological improvement that affects all varieties, both the domestic output of the product (including that part that is exported) and imports of it increase.

I include both the exports and imports of each industry in the regressions as appropriate in this environment rather than just the industry differences between these two variables (i.e., net exports). Thus, the analysis here properly does not impose the condition that the employment effect of a given increase in an industry's exports is the same (but the opposite in sign) as an equivalent increase in the industry's imports (as would be appropriate if the goods were perfect substitutes and the markets were perfectly competitive).

Summary Statistics

Table 5.1 reports the industry mean and standard deviation of the various dependent (left-hand-side) and independent (right-hand-side) variables used in the regression analysis of the 74 industries making up the manufacturing sector for the periods 1977–87 and 1987–97. Table 5.2 does the same for those industries included in the combined goods and services industry grouping in which there are both imports and exports at the outset of the period covered.

Among the relationships brought out in tables 5.1 and 5.2 are the significant declines in union membership in both the 1977–87 and 1987–97 periods, especially during the first period and particularly in manufacturing industries, in contrast to sizable increases in the employment of nonunion workers, especially in services. As was noted above, the decline in union membership occurred largely among workers with a high school education or less, with unionization among individuals with more education actually increasing except in manufacturing between 1977 and

Table 5.1 Summary statistics for manufacturing, 1977–87 and 1987–97

Variable	Period	Industry mean[a]	Standard deviation[a]
Dependent variables			
Industry change in employment (thousands of workers)			
All	1977–87	−10.69	80.92
	1987–97	8.63	71.01
Union	1977–87	−35.73	46.88
	1987–97	−15.59	21.94
Nonunion	1977–87	25.04	67.72
	1987–97	24.22	62.94
Basically educated union	1977–87	−34.50	43.41
	1987–97	−16.79	20.91
Basically educated nonunion	1977–87	1.27	39.18
	1987–97	1.02	38.18
More-educated union	1977–87	−1.46	7.47
	1987–97	1.20	9.02
More-educated nonunion	1977–87	22.03	43.64
	1987–97	23.20	42.02
Independent variables			
Industry change in output components (billions of 1987 dollars)			
Change in domestic spending	1977–87	6.58	13.05
	1987–97	26.26	107.12
Change in imports	1977–87	2.72	6.20
	1987–97	8.77	37.04
Change in exports	1977–87	0.74	2.49
	1987–97	2.49	4.07
Change in labor coefficients (thousands of workers per 1 billion 1987 dollars of industry shipments)			
All workers	1977–87	−2.74	7.10
	1987–97	−1.35	2.29
Basically educated workers	1977–97	−1.54	1.68
More-educated workers	1977–87	−0.20	4.56
	1987–97	0.19	1.18

a. Based on 74 manufacturing industries.

Source: Author's calculations.

Table 5.2 Summary statistics for goods and services sectors, 1977-87 and 1987-97

Variable	Period	Sector or industry mean[a]	Standard deviation[a]
Dependent variables Sector or industry change in employment (thousands of workers)			
All	1977–87	14.42	149.66
	1987–97	58.30	224.49
Union	1977–87	−33.57	49.27
	1987–97	−11.86	39.56
Nonunion	1977–87	47.99	133.97
	1987–97	70.16	211.69
Basically educated union	1977–87	−33.74	43.99
	1987–97	−15.37	20.90
Basically educated nonunion	1977–87	5.22	71.34
	1987–97	7.93	89.41
More-educated union	1977–87	0.00	11.32
	1987–97	3.52	28.31
More-educated nonunion	1977–87	41.36	84.81
	1987–97	62.23	145.37
Independent variables Sector or industry change in output components (billions of 1987 dollars)			
Change in domestic spending	1977–87	7.16	19.27
	1987–97	23.84	96.65
Change in imports	1977–87	2.04	7.04
	1987–97	7.41	32.65
Change in exports	1977–87	.70	2.44
	1987–97	2.48	4.06
Change in sector or industry labor coefficient (thousands of workers per 1 billion 1987 dollars)			
All workers	1977–87	−2.24	7.08
	1987–97	−1.35	6.25
Basically educated workers	1977–87	−2.33	3.13
	1987–97	−1.57	2.41
More-educated workers	1977–87	0.09	4.41
	1987–97	0.22	4.28

a. Based on 74 manufacturing, 12 services, and 6 primary-product industries.
   Based on 74 manufacturing, 17 services, and 6 primary-product industries.

Source: Author's calculations.

1987. The considerable worsening of the US trade balance, especially between 1987 and 1997, is also clearly shown in the tables.

Another variable of interest is the change in the average industry labor coefficient (i.e., l_i), the average number of workers (in thousands) employed per $1 billion of shipments in the industries included in the data set. In table 5.2, the labor coefficient decreases for all workers of 2.24 and 1.35 for the 1977–87 and 1987–97 periods, respectively, for the goods and services industries in the dataset represent declines of 20 and 13 percent, respectively. The labor coefficient can decrease both because of labor-saving technological changes and because of increases in wages relative to the returns to nonlabor productive factors, the latter development bringing about the substitution of capital and other factors for labor. Because the decreases are mainly in the labor coefficients for less-educated labor (with the coefficient for more-educated workers actually rising in one of the periods) and the wages of less-educated workers fell significantly relative to those of more-educated workers in both periods, technological changes appear to be the main cause of the decline in labor coefficients.

Regression Results

The results of the regression analysis are presented in tables 5.3 to 5.7. The analysis proceeds in three stages. First, tables 5.3 and 5.4 report the partial regression coefficients from regressing changes in domestic expenditures, imports, exports, and labor coefficients across industries on both changes in the number of union workers and changes in the number of nonunion workers during two periods, 1977–87 and 1987–97. The regressions are run separately for two sets of industries: first, for manufacturing industries alone, and then for manufacturing industries plus all agricultural, mining, and services industries in which there are both imports and exports (traded goods and services) during the period covered.

Table 5.3 reports the estimated regression coefficients for the four independent variables and the constant term for the eight separate regression equations involved in these combinations of changes in union workers and nonunion workers during the two periods and for the two sets of industries. Table 5.3 also reports the standard errors associated with the estimated coefficients (and the levels of statistical significance that these indicate), a measure of the overall significance of the regressions (F-statistic), a measure of the regression equation's goodness of fit (R^2), and the number of industries included in each regression.

Table 5.4 shows comparable regression results at an even finer level of industry detail, namely, dividing union and nonunion workers in each industry into those who are basically educated (12 or fewer years of schooling) and those who are more-educated (13 or more years of schooling).

Table 5.3 Employment changes by union status regressed on changes in domestic spending, imports, exports, and labor coefficients, 1977–87 and 1987–97

Union status	Domestic spending	Imports	Exports	Labor coefficient	Constant	R^2	F-statistic
Manufactured goods[d]							
Union workers							
1977–87	1.70[a]	−6.84[a]	3.14	0.08	−30.44[a]	0.49	16.45
	(0.51)	(0.89)	(2.73)	(0.82)	(4.64)		
1987–97	1.14[a]	−3.23[a]	−2.30[a]	2.02[b]	−8.82[a]	0.43	13.14
	(0.21)	(0.60)	(0.65)	(0.96)	(2.56)		
Nonunion workers							
1977–87	5.62[a]	−4.45[a]	2.99	3.26[a]	6.88	0.68	36.02
	(0.59)	(1.02)	(3.13)	(0.94)	(5.33)		
1987–97	3.77[a]	−10.87[a]	6.74[a]	8.40[a]	15.14[a]	0.66	33.51
	(0.47)	(1.34)	(1.44)	(2.13)	(5.69)		
Traded goods and services[e]							
Union workers							
1977–87	0.75[b]	−3.76[a]	6.23[b]	1.11	−33.12[a]	0.26	7.55
	(0.30)	(0.77)	(2.50)	(0.81)	(4.88)		
1987–97	−0.09	0.20	−0.49	1.51[b]	−8.07[c]	0.08	1.94
	(0.15)	(0.45)	(1.24)	(0.71)	(4.83)		
Nonunion workers							
1977–87	3.27[a]	−3.31[c]	24.77[a]	11.82[a]	40.44[a]	0.43	16.40
	(0.71)	(1.85)	(5.96)	(1.94)	(11.79)		
1987–97	2.71[a]	−8.28[a]	8.50	−2.09	43.04	0.17	4.68
	(0.77)	(2.27)	(6.30)	(3.62)	(24.51)		

a. Coefficients significantly different from zero at the 1 percent level.
b. Coefficients significantly different from zero at the 5 percent level.
c. Coefficients significantly different from zero at the 10 percent level.
d. The number of observations of manufactured goods for all years was 74.
e. The number of observations for traded goods and services in 1977–87 was 92, and for 1987–97 was 97.

Note: Numbers in parentheses are standard errors.

Source: See appendix A.

Including this education factor with the other industry characteristics yields the 16 regression results reported in table 5.4.

For the second stage of the regression analysis, table 5.5 presents calculations indicating whether the expected negative (or positive) impact of import (or export) increases on union and nonunion workers are proportional to the relative number of union and nonunion workers employed across the industries at the outset of a period. When import

Table 5.4 Employment changes by education level and union status regressed on changes in domestic spending, imports, exports, and labor coefficients, 1977–87 and 1987–97

Union status	Domestic spending	Imports	Exports	Labor coefficient	Constant	R^2	F-statistic
Manufactured goods[d]							
Basically educated union workers							
1977–87	1.17[b]	−6.13[a]	2.84	−0.46	−28.80[a]	0.48	15.95
	(0.48)	(0.83)	(2.22)	(1.60)	(5.18)		
1987–97	0.61[a]	−1.63[a]	−3.60[a]	2.69[b]	−5.54[c]	0.44	13.45
	(0.20)	(0.58)	(0.62)	(1.17)	(2.80)		
Basically educated nonunion workers							
1977–87	2.39[a]	−2.39[a]	2.98	7.43[a]	8.58[c]	0.44	13.28
	(0.04)	(0.78)	(2.09)	(1.51)	(4.87)		
1987–97	2.29[a]	−6.66[a]	1.07	7.62[a]	8.30[c]	0.55	21.34
	(0.33)	(0.94)	(1.00)	(1.90)	(4.56)		
More-educated union workers							
1977–87	0.43[a]	−0.6[a]	0.95[c]	0.67[a]	−3.2[a]	0.43	12.89
	(0.09)	(0.15)	(0.48)	(0.22)	(0.78)		
1987–97	0.50[a]	−1.53[a]	1.31[a]	1.60[b]	−2.15[b]	0.62	27.67
	(0.07)	(0.20)	(0.22)	(0.67)	(0.84)		
More-educated nonunion workers							
1977–87	3.04[a]	−1.65[b]	2.73	2.69[a]	5.04	0.66	33.99
	(0.38)	0.65	(2.06)	(0.94)	(3.35)		
1987–97	1.52[a]	−4.25[a]	5.84[a]	14.40[a]	3.35	0.57	23.28
	(0.33)	(0.94)	(1.03)	(3.12)	(3.92)		
Traded goods and services[e]							
Basically educated union workers							
1977–87	0.57[b]	−3.64[a]	4.1[b]	1.62	−29.51[a]	0.27	8.02
	(0.27)	(0.69)	(2.02)	(1.48)	(5.09)		
1987–97	0.04	−0.04	−2.28	2.31[a]	−6.66[b]	0.21	5.85
	(0.07)	(0.21)	(0.61)	(0.86)	(2.70)		
Basically educated nonunion workers							
1977–87	0.44	−0.28	13.22[a]	14.24[a]	26.56[a]	0.34	11.13
	(0.41)	(1.06)	(3.11)	(2.29)	(7.86)		

(table continues next page)

Table 5.4 Employment changes by education level and union status regressed on changes in domestic spending, imports, exports, and labor coefficients, 1977–87 and 1987–97 (*continued*)

Union status	Domestic spending	Imports	Exports	Labor coefficient	Constant	R^2	F-statistic
Basically educated nonunion workers							
1987–97	0.89[a]	−2.69[a]	0.99	−4.09	−2.22	0.11	2.96
	(0.32)	(0.96)	(2.73)	(3.89)	(12.18)		
More-educated union workers							
1977–87	0.17[b]	−0.09	2.53[a]	1.17[a]	−2.92[a]	0.32	10.11
	(0.07)	(0.17)	(0.57)	(0.30)	(1.11)		
1987–97	−0.12	0.25	1.8[b]	1.16	−0.08	0.12	3.25
	(0.11)	(0.31)	(0.87)	(0.73)	(3.28)		
More-educated nonunion workers							
1977–87	2.8[a]	−2.88[a]	10.25[a]	9.29[a]	19.14[b]	0.44	0.59
	(0.45)	1.15	(3.87)	(2.00)	(7.15)		
1987–97	1.87[a]	−5.71[a]	7.37	−0.5	41.87[b]	0.16	4.51
	(0.53)	(1.60)	(4.34)	(3.66)	(16.44)		

a. Coefficients significantly different from zero at the 1 percent level.
b. Coefficients significantly different from zero at the 5 percent level.
c. Coefficients significantly different from zero at the 10 percent level.
d. The number of observations of manufactured goods for all years was 74.
e. The number of observations for traded goods and services in 1977–87 was 92, and for 1987–97 was 97.

Note: Numbers in parentheses are standard errors.

Source: See appendix A.

increases are neutral in their impact on union versus nonunion workers, unionist displacement shares correspond to unionist employment shares.

In this case of neutrality, one expects the estimated regression coefficient for the negative impact on the number of union workers of (say) a $1 billion increase in imports of manufactured goods to be less than the negative impact on the number of nonunion workers associated with this import increase, simply because the number of union workers in the typical manufacturing industry, for example, is less than the number of nonunion workers. Under these circumstances, the ratio of union to nonunion workers negatively affected in employment terms should be approximately equal to the ratio of union to nonunion workers employed in the industries covered.

Table 5.5 Comparison of initial ratios of union to nonunion employment and ratios of changes in union to nonunion employment associated with trade changes and education level, 1977–87 and 1987–97

Education level and period	Employment ratio at beginning of period	Ratio of changes associated with:	
		Changes in imports	Changes in exports
All levels of education			
Manufacturing			
1977–87	0.61	**1.54**[a]	1.05
1987–97	0.33	0.30	**−0.34**[a]
Traded goods and services			
1977–87	0.47	**1.14**[c]	0.25
1987–97	0.23	*−0.02*[a]	−0.06
12 or fewer years of education			
Manufacturing			
1977–87	0.75	**2.56**[a]	0.95
1987–97	0.43	*0.24*[c]	**−3.38**[a]
Traded goods and services			
1977–87	0.58	**12.89**[a]	0.31
1987–97	0.30	*0.02*[b]	**−2.32**[a]
13 or more years of education			
Manufacturing			
1977–87	0.30	0.36	0.35
1987–97	0.18	**0.36**[a]	0.22
Traded goods and services			
1977–87	0.25	*0.03*[b]	0.24
1987–97	0.16	*−0.04*[a]	0.30

a. Difference between ratio of employment changes of union to nonunion workers significantly different from ratio of total employment of union to nonunion workers at the 1 percent level.
b. Difference between ratio of employment changes of union to nonunion workers significantly different from ratio of total employment of union to nonunion workers at the 5 percent level.
c. Difference between ratio of employment changes of union to nonunion workers significantly different from ratio of total employment of union to nonunion workers at the 10 percent level.

Note: Ratios of union to nonunion import changes indicating that union workers fared relatively worse in a statistically significant sense than nonunion workers are displayed in bold type, whereas those indicating that union workers fared relatively better in a statistically significant sense than nonunion workers are displayed in bold italics.

Source: Author's calculations.

A ratio of the numbers of union to nonunion workers (where both groups are negatively affected by increased imports) that is statistically significantly larger than the average ratio of union to nonunion employment suggests that unionist displacement is extraordinarily and disproportionately high.[6] It would be consistent with such hypotheses as that increased management opposition to unions induced by decreased profit opportunities brought about by increased import competition resulted in a disproportionately adverse employment-adjustment impact for union workers. In contrast, a positive ratio of union to nonunion displacement impact that is less than the ratio of union to nonunion employment indicates that union workers are relatively less adversely affected than nonunion workers by increased imports.

On the export side, a ratio of the increase in employment of union to the increase in nonunion workers associated with a $1 billion increase in exports smaller (or larger) than the ratio of the number of union to nonunion workers employed in the covered industries indicates that union workers did not fare as well as nonunion workers (or fared better than nonunion workers) in relative terms from the positive employment impact of increased exports.

In the third stage of the regression analysis, even if the relationships of these ratios indicate that union workers are more adversely affected in employment terms than nonunion workers by increases in imports or exports, one needs to determine if this differential trade effect represents a major or minor component of the unionization decline in the industries covered in the analysis. Tables 5.6 and 5.7 (on p. 58 and p. 61) provide the information relevant to this question by using the estimated regression coefficients on the changes in domestic expenditures, imports, exports, labor coefficients, and the constant term together with the actual industry changes in these variables to allocate the total changes in the number of union and nonunion workers among the four independent variables and a constant term. The constant term picks up the employment effects brought about by variables not included in the regression equations, such as a general antiunion shift in behavior toward unions by management and antiunion governmental actions, as were discussed in chapter 1.

To begin with, consider the manner in which the estimated regression coefficients in tables 5.3 and 5.4 (on p. 46 and p. 47) should be interpreted and some of the main differences in their signs and magnitudes across industry groups, time periods, and union versus nonunion status. The set of coefficients listed in the first row of table 5.3 covers all unionized

---

6. As is discussed below, when the changes in either union or nonunion employment are unexpectedly positive when imports increase so that their ratio is negative, the matter of which group fares relatively better obviously depends simply on which of the two groups has the positive sign. The same point applies when the change in employment from increased exports is negative for either union or nonunion employment.

workers in the 74 manufacturing industries in the data set during the period 1977–87. As is shown in the imports and exports columns, for example, they indicate that a $1 billion increase in imports (all other variables remaining unchanged) is, on average, associated with a decrease in industry employment of 6.84 thousand union workers, or, expressed in numbers of workers per $1 billion, 6,840 union workers, and a $1 billion rise in exports with an increase of 3.14 thousand union workers per industry, i.e., 3,140 union workers. A $1 billion rise in domestic spending is associated with an industry rise in union employment of 1,700 workers, whereas the average industry change during the period in the labor input coefficient (i.e., the number of workers used to produce $1 billion worth of output) is associated with a decline in union employment of 80 workers.

Other influences picked up by the constant term in the regression equation are associated with an average employment decrease in each industry from 1977 to 1987 of 30,440 workers. It should be emphasized that these numbers do not represent actual changes in the number of jobs, but are best viewed as short-run adjustment-pressure effects, holding the other variables constant.

The expected negative relationship between changes in imports and changes in employment and positive relationships between changes in domestic expenditures, exports, and labor coefficients and changes in employment generally hold for union and union workers during both periods and sets of industries in table 5.3. The only deviation from this sign pattern occurs for the export-change coefficient of union workers as a group during the 1987–97 period in both the manufacturing sector and the traded goods and services industry group. The export signs are negative, and the coefficient is statistically significant in the manufacturing sector.

Table 5.4 (on p. 47) in which union workers are divided into those who are basically educated (12 or fewer years of education) and those who are more-educated (13 or more years of schooling), indicates that the basically educated group of union workers is the source of the statistically significant negative export coefficient on all union workers in this time period. The export coefficient on more-educated union workers for the 1987–97 time period is significantly positive in both manufacturing and the traded goods and services group. Table 5.4 also shows an unexpectedly negative sign for the regression coefficient on the labor coefficient-change variable for basically educated workers in the 1977–87 period. An important feature of the constant term in the various equations for both time periods is that it is negative for unionized workers but positive for nonunion employees.

About three-quarters of all the regression coefficients in table 5.3 differ from zero in a statistically significant manner. But there is a considerably higher proportion of significant variables in the manufacturing sector alone (80 percent) compared with the traded goods and services group (65 percent). This occurs because excluding the 74 manufacturing industries from the data set used for the regressions and regressing the independent variables only on changes in the numbers of union and nonunion workers employed in those nonmanufacturing industries with both imports and exports (18 in the 1977–87 period and 23 in the 1987–97 period) generally yields insignificant coefficients (a number of which have the wrong signs) for the import-change and export-change variables.[7]

The regression coefficients for the other two independent variables (changes in domestic spending and in labor coefficients) also have unexpected signs in the nonmanufacturing regressions, especially for union workers. Because these outcomes could be consequences either of poor data for many of the nonmanufacturing industries or of diverse omitted variables affecting these industries, we shall emphasize the regression results covering manufacturing for which the quality of data seems much better and the forces affecting the coefficients are more uniform across sectors.

As was stressed above, a key issue being investigated in the regression analysis is whether increases in imports and exports affected the employment of union workers and nonunion workers in a comparable manner. This can be ascertained for workers engaged in manufacturing activities during the 1977–87 period, for example, by comparing the relative magnitudes of the import and export coefficients for union and nonunion workers engaged in manufacturing (reported in the first and third rows of regression coefficients in table 5.3) with the relative number of union and nonunion workers employed in manufacturing at the outset of the period. The coefficient for the import-change variable for union workers in the 1977–87 period implies, as was pointed out above, that a $1 billion increase in industry imports for the 74 manufacturing industries is, on average, associated with a decrease in employment of 6,840 union workers, whereas the import-change coefficient for nonunion workers in manufacturing during this period indicates an average industry decrease in nonunion employment of only 4,450 jobs.

Because there were more nonunion than union workers in manufacturing in 1977, these estimates suggest that relative to nonunionized manufacturing workers, unionized workers were disproportionately affected in an adverse manner by import growth. The ratio of the industry decrease in 6,840 union jobs to the industry decrease in 4,450 nonunion jobs per $1 billion rise in imports in manufacturing during the 1977–87 period is 1.54. In contrast, the ratio of total employment in manufacturing of all union workers to total employment of all nonunion workers in this sector in 1977 is only 0.61.[8] Moreover, the ratio of change

---

7. These regressions are not reported in the tables but are available from the author.

8. This is the case because, as reported in table 2.1, the proportion of unionized workers in manufacturing in 1977 was 38.0 percent and thus the 1977 proportion of nonunionized workers in manufacturing was 62.0 percent. Consequently, the ratio of union to nonunion workers was 38.0/62.0, or 0.61.

in union to nonunion employment per $1 billion of imports in manu
turing between 1977 and 1987 differs from the ratio of total employm
of union to nonunion workers in 1977 at the 1 percent level of statisti
significance.[9]

The ratio of the export-change coefficients for union and nonunion
workers in manufacturing during this period is +3,140 union workers
per $1 billion divided by +2,990 nonunion workers per $1 billion (see
table 5.3), or 1.05. Because of this export-side ratio is positive, it indicates that a $1 billion rise in exports created relatively more jobs for
union workers than would be expected from their relative importance in
manufacturing at the period's outset. However, the difference between
the 1.05 union–nonunion export ratio and the 0.61 union–nonunion employment ratio in manufacturing is not statistically significant at a level
of 10 percent or less.

To facilitate such comparisons, table 5.5 (on p. 49) indicates the ratios
of the employment of union to nonunion workers in manufacturing alone
and in the combined traded goods and services product group at the
beginning of each period for workers at all levels of education as well as
for basically educated and more educated workers. It also reports the
ratios of the regression coefficients of the changes in union to the changes
in nonunion employment associated with a $1 billion increase in imports
as well as for exports.

Table 5.5 also indicates whether the ratios of the changes in union to
nonunion employment differ at conventional levels of statistical significance from the corresponding ratios of the employment of union to nonunion members. To facilitate the interpretations to be given to the comparisons, union to nonunion import-change ratios indicating that union
workers fared relatively worse in a statistically significant sense than
nonunion workers are displayed in bold print, whereas those indicating
that union workers fared relatively better in a statistically significant sense
than nonunion workers are displayed in bold italics.

---

9. This significance level is measured by first calculating the differences between the
changes in the number of union workers across manufacturing industries between the
1977–87 (let this be nun7787) and the changes in the number of nonunion workers
acrossmanufacturing industries between 1977–87 (let this be nno7787), where the latter
numbers are each multiplied by the ratio of the total number of union to total number of
nonunion workers in manufacturing in 1977 (let this constant term be tnun77/tnno77).
Expressed as an equation, the differences calculated across manufacturing industries are
nno7787 − (nno7787*tnun77/tnno77). These differences are then regressed on the usual
right-hand-side variables in the regression equation, namely, changes in domestic spending, imports, exports, and labor coefficients across manufacturing industries during the
1977–87 period. Finally, the level at which the import coefficient (or any of the other
coefficients) is statistically different from zero is then determined. A similar procedure
for determining statistical significance with regard to the ratios of changes of union
to nonunion workers associated with import changes is followed for other groups of
workers and sets of industries as well as for exports.

Consider first the relationships between the employment ratios and the two trade ratios during the 1977–87 decade, beginning with the basically educated (12 or fewer years of education) group of workers (shown in the middle rows of table 5.5), along with the more-educated workers (13 or more years of education, in the bottom rows), and finally both groups combined (in the top rows). The most important conclusion to be drawn on the import side from table 5.5 in this period is that basically educated union workers fared worse in a statistically significant sense compared with basically educated nonunion workers, both in the manufacturing and in the combined traded goods and services industry groups. The ratio of the number of basically educated to more-educated workers employed in manufacturing in 1977 is 0.75, whereas the statistically significant ratio of the decrease in the number basically educated workers to more-educated workers per $1 billion increase in imports during the 1977–87 period is 2.56. For traded goods and services as a product group, the same ratios are 0.58 and 12.89, respectively.

For more-educated union workers alone, the relationships during the 1977–87 period are rather different than for the basically educated group. More-educated union workers were affected in employment terms in about the same relative manner as more-educated nonunion workers in the manufacturing sector and in a better (and statistically significant) manner in the traded goods and services sector. Specifically, for this education category, the ratio of union to nonunion employment change for manufacturing imports is about the same (0.36) as the ratio of union to nonunion total employment (0.30); but the ratio of union to nonunion employment change for imports of traded goods and services is considerably smaller (0.03) when compared with a 1977 total employment ratio of 0.25.

Because the number of basically educated workers is considerably larger than the number of more-educated workers, the relationships for all workers (union plus nonunion) as a group are the same as for the basically educated group. The 1977–87 ratio of the negative employment-adjustment impact on manufacturing of a $1 billion increase in imports on union compared with nonunion workers is 1.54 and differs in a statistically significant manner, whereas in that sector the ratio of the total employment of union to nonunion workers in 1977 for all levels of education is only 0.61. In the traded goods and services product group, the respective ratios are 1.14 and 0.47.

On the export side for the 1977–87 period, no significant relationships exists with regard to how well union workers fared compared with nonunion workers in employment-creation terms. The ratio of all union to all nonunion jobs associated with a $1 billion increase in exports in the manufacturing sector is 1.05, compared with a 1977 total employment ratio for these workers of 0.61.

Although this indicates a more favorable employment treatment of all union relative to all nonunion workers, the difference between these ratios is not statistically significant. For both basically educated and more-educated employees in manufacturing, the employment-increase ratios for union relative to nonunion workers are also greater than the total employment ratio, but again the differences are not statistically significant. For the traded goods and services group during the 1977–87 period, the union to nonunion employment-change ratios are all higher than the total employment ratios (indicating that union workers fared relatively worse than nonunion workers); but again, the ratios do not differ in a statistically significant sense.

Next, consider the relationships between these ratios for the three worker-groups during the 1987–97 period. They are quite different from the 1977–87 period on both the import and export sides. With regard to import increases, the most striking relationship is that basically educated union workers fared relatively better in employment displacement terms than basically educated nonunion workers. In contrast to the first period, the 1987–97 ratios of employment decreases of union and nonunion workers associated with increased imports are smaller (rather than larger) in a statistically significant sense for basically educated workers than the employment ratio of basically educated union to nonunion workers in 1987 in both manufacturing and traded goods and services, namely, 0.24 to 0.43 and 0.02 to 0.30, respectively. Furthermore, whereas in the 1977–87 period more-educated union workers in manufacturing fared relatively about the same as more-educated nonunion workers, in the 1987–97 period more-educated union workers in the manufacturing sector fared relatively worse in statistically significant terms than more-educated nonunion workers.

The negative signs on the union to nonunion employment-change ratios associated with increased imports in the traded goods and services industry group both for all workers as a group and for more educated workers are the consequence of positive (rather than the expected negative) regression coefficients on the union worker variable for these two groups of workers (see tables 5.3 and 5.5). These positive coefficients are not statistically different from zero, however. But when the employment-change ratios are compared with the total employment ratios for these groups of workers, they do differ in a statistically significant sense. They indicate a more favorable treatment in the goods and services sector during the 1987–97 period for all union workers as a group compared with all nonunion workers and for more-educated union workers compared with their nonunion counterparts.

On the export side, the union to nonunion employment-change ratios for 1987–97 not only have a negative (rather than the expected positive) sign in four of the six cases but differ statistically from their 1987 overall employment ratios of union to nonunion workers at the 1 percent level in three of these cases. This is the consequence of the negative relationship between changes in exports and changes in the employment of basically educated union workers (but not basically educated nonunion or more educated union and nonunion ones) that exists in the regression results for the 1987–97 period (see table 5.4).[11] For example, a $1 billion increase in exports is associated with the loss of 3,600 jobs for basically educated union workers in the manufacturing sector.[12]

The most likely reason for this relationship would seem to be that the increases in exports are correlated with some economic factor not explicitly included in the regression equation that has the effect of decreasing the employment of basically educated workers. One plausible factor is foreign direct investment, which we know is positively correlated with exports (see Lipsey, forthcoming), and which in recent years has been associated with the transfer of less-skill-intensive production activities from the United States to lower-wage countries.[13] The existence of the wage premium earned by union workers (see table 2.4), coupled with greater competitive pressures in export markets than domestic markets, may account for increased foreign direct investment by firms directed at producing less-skill-intensive components abroad in certain industries and thus for the negative relationship between export changes and

---

11. The negative signs of the union to nonunion employment-change ratios for all workers in manufacturing alone and in all traded goods and services are, for example, due to the influence of the negative 1987–97 relationship between increases in exports and the change in the number of basically educated workers employed in these product groups, because increases in exports and changes in the employment of more-educated workers are positively related (see table 5.4).

12. A scatter diagram of the partial regression coefficients of increases in exports and changes in the employment of basically educated union labor across manufacturing industries indicates that the industries responsible for the negative export coefficient are the manufacturing industries 61–81 in the list of industries in appendix B. These industries include such products as machinery and computing equipment; electrical machinery, equipment, and supplies; transportation equipment; professional photographic equipment and watches; and amusement and sporting equipment. Regressing the independent variables for the other manufacturing industries, namely, industries 8–60, yields a significantly positive coefficient for the export-change coefficient. Moreover, whereas the constant term is significantly negative in the 8–60 group of industries (as is the case for all manufacturing industries as a group), the constant term is positive, although not significant, for manufacturing industries 61–81.

13. Export increases seem to be positively associated with increases in foreign direct investment for a number of reasons. When a firm outsources less-skill-intensive production activities to foreign countries, the outsourcing activities often take place on a skill-intensive production component that is produced domestically and then exported. Moreover, if the final product is sold in third countries, it is often less expensive to ship other skill-intensive components to the outsourcing country for final assembly rather than shipping the unskilled labor–intensive component back to the home country to be assembled with the other components and then exported to the third countries. Even when the unskilled labor–intensive part is exported to the home country, the savings in labor costs may enable the firm to increase its exports of the final product as it becomes more competitive internationally.

employment changes of basically educated union workers in the 1987–97 decade.[14]

As was discussed in chapter 4, the fact that foreign outsourcing often involves exports of skilled labor–intensive components on which unskilled labor-intensive tasks are undertaken also contributes directly to this negative relationship between export increases and the employment of basically educated union workers. Of course, simply poor measurement of these variables may also account for this result. We clearly need to make testing efforts—both with a more complex econometric model that includes measures of the fundamental economic forces affecting trade and employment and with a more detailed database—before we can be confident about the validity of our findings on this matter.

Total Employment Effects

Whereas tables 5.3 and 5.4 indicate the estimated employment effects per $1 billion change in domestic spending, imports, and exports and per unit change in labor coefficients, tables 5.6 and 5.7 report the changes in total employment associated with the actual changes in these variables—that is, the employment changes obtained by multiplying the regression coefficients in tables 5.3 and 5.5 by the respective observed changes across industries in the right-hand-side variables.[15] This provides information concerning the relative importance in total employment terms for union and nonunion workers of the different right-hand-side variables and the constant term.

For example, table 5.6 indicates that the increase in domestic spending on manufactured goods during the 1977–87 period was associated with an adjustment impact on union workers of all education levels who are employed in manufacturing of +828,000 workers. The change in union employment associated with the increase in imports during this period was –1,374,000 jobs, whereas the change in the employment of union workers in this sector related to the increase in exports was +172,000 workers. The decline in the number of workers required per $1 billion of industry output resulted in a change in union workers of –17,000. The employment-impact importance of factors other than changes in domestic

---

14. The existence of a positive (though not statistically significant) regression coefficient for basically educated nonunion workers (see table 5.4) suggests that employers may have used the threat of transferring production activities abroad as a means of inducing basically educated union workers to drop their union affiliation.

15. Because of rounding, the sum of the employment changes in tables 5.6 and 5.7 for workers of different educational levels and in different product groups may not exactly equal the product of the industry means of number of workers multiplied by the number of industries that are reported in tables 5.1 and 5.2.

Table 5.6 Estimated employment changes by union status associated with changes in domestic spending, imports, exports, and labor coefficients, 1977–87 and 1987–97 (thousands of workers)

Union status	Domestic spending	Imports	Exports	Labor coefficient	Other factors	Total change
Manufactured goods						
Union workers						
1977–87	828	−1,374	172	−17	−2,252	−2,643
1987–97	2,218	−2,094	−424	−202	−653	−1,155
Nonunion workers						
1977–87	2,736	−895	164	−661	509	1,853
1987–97	7,319	−7,053	1,243	−838	1,120	1,781
Traded goods and services						
Union workers						
1977–87	492	−707	403	−229	−3,047	−3,047
1987–97	−194	137	−118	−197	−782	−782
Nonunion workers						
1977–87	2,156	−622	1,600	−2,449	3,721	3,721
1987–97	6,264	−5,949	2,043	273	4,175	4,175

Source: Author's calculations.

spending, imports, exports, and the labor coefficients that are picked up by the constant term in the regression is indicated by the change of −2,252,000 union workers associated with this term.

The sum of all these changes, namely, −2,643,000 union workers, is equal to the change in union membership in manufacturing during the 1977–87 period. The employment-impact effects for nonunion workers in manufacturing during this period associated with the four independent variables are +2,736,000 nonunion workers from domestic spending, −895,000 from imports, +164,000 from exports, and −661,000 from the change in labor coefficients. In contrast to union workers, the effect of omitted variables on the employment of nonunion workers is positive, namely, +509,000 nonunion workers. The sum of the employment adjustment impact on nonunion workers of the independent variables and the omitted variables is +1,853,000.

Of special interest with regard to these estimates of short-run adjustment impact is the relative importance of any differential treatment of union versus nonunion workers associated with changes in trade in accounting for the overall decline in unionization. As was pointed out in the previous section (see table 5.5), there is statistically significant evidence that the employment adjustment effects of increased imports in the manufacturing sector during the 1977–87 period did negatively affected basically educated union workers in a manner that was greater than their relative importance in the manufacturing labor force. Specifically, the ratio of the employment impact of –1,374,000 union jobs compared with –895,000 nonunion jobs, namely, 1.54, associated with increased imports during this period (see table 5.6) is much greater than the ratio of union to nonunion workers in the manufacturing sector at the outset of the period, namely, 0.61.

The magnitude of the disproportionately adverse impact of increased imports on union workers can be estimated as the difference between the –1,374,000 and what this number would be if the sum of the negative employment impact of increased imports on union plus nonunion employment during the period (–1,374,000 plus –895,000, or –2,269,000 workers) is allocated in proportion to the 0.61 ratio of union to nonunion workers employed in manufacturing in 1977. If this estimating procedure is followed, the negative impact of increased imports on union employment versus nonunion workers amounts to –860,000 union workers instead of –1,374,000 union workers.[16] Thus, the measure of the disproportionately adverse impact of increased imports on union workers amounts to –514,000 union workers (–1,374,000 minus –860,000). Although this is a substantial number of workers, the discriminatory employment impact of increases in imports of manufactured goods on union compared with nonunion workers is equal to less than one-quarter of the negative impact on union members of influences not captured by the independent variables in the regression equation but, instead, indicated by the constant term of –2,252,000 union workers.[17] This implies that factors other than the extent of import increases across industries played the dominant role in accounting for the decline in union employment during the period.

If similar calculations are undertaken for the 1977–87 change in union membership in manufacturing for basically educated workers by themselves (see table 5.7), the discriminatory impact of increased imports in the manufacturing sector on the employment of union compared with

---

16. Let x and y equal the hypothetical employment effects of increased imports on union and nonunion workers, respectively, in manufacturing if the total decrease in the employment of union and nonunion workers associated with increased imports in 1977–87 (–1,374,000 plus –895,000 = –2,269,000; see table 5.7) is distributed in the same ratio as the total number of union to nonunion workers employed in manufacturing in 1977, namely, 0.61 (see table 5.5). Thus, solving the two equations, $x/y = 0.61$ and $x + y = -2,269,000$, yields values for x and y of –860,000 and –1,409,000, respectively. The difference between the calculated value for basically educated union workers in table 5.7 (–1,374,00) and the hypothetical value for basically educated ones (–850,000) is –514,000.

17. Another indicator of the importance of the "other factors" not included among the independent variables in "explaining" the change in union membership in the 1977–87 period is that the combined impact of changes in all the independent variables, namely, changes in domestic expenditures, imports, exports and labor coefficients, account for only –391,000 of the total change in union membership of –2,643,000.

nonunion workers amounts to –498,000 workers, a number that again is equal to less than a quarter of the negative employment impact of omitted variables, namely, –2,132,000 basically educated union workers.[18]

As was also noted in discussing table 5.5 and in contrast to the 1977–87 period, there is statistically significant evidence in the 1987–97 period that increased imports affected the employment of basically educated union workers in a less (rather than more) negative manner than would be expected from their relative importance in overall employment terms. If the negative employment impact on basically educated union workers plus the negative impact on nonunion workers of increased imports in manufacturing during the 1987–97 period (see table 5.7) of –1,055,000 plus –4,324,000 or –5,379,000 workers had been distributed in proportion to the 0.43 employment ratio (see table 5.5) of basically educated union to basically educated nonunion workers in manufacturing for 1987, the negative employment impact of the increased imports on union workers would have been –1,617,000 rather than the –1,055,000 number reported in table 5.7.[19] The difference between –1,055,000 and –1,617,000, namely +562,000 workers, is a measure of the relatively less adverse (i.e., more favorable) employment effect of increased imports on basically educated union compared with basically educated nonunion workers in the 1987–97 decade.

At the same time, I also find that export increases were associated with an unexpected, statistically significant decrease in the employment of basically educated union workers in manufacturing during the 1987–97 decade. As is reported in table 5.7, the estimated magnitude of this change is –665,000 basically educated workers in the manufacturing sector, whereas the estimated change in the number of basically educated

---

18. As is indicated in table 5.7, the negative employment impact of increased imports on basically educated union workers in manufacturing in 1977–87 is –1,232,000, and the negative impact on basically educated nonunion workers is –480,000, thus yielding a –1,712,000 change in all basically educated manufacturing workers associated with import increases during this period. The ratio of basically educated union workers to basically educated nonunion workers in 1977 is 0.75 (see table 5.5). Thus, the negative impact on basically educated unionized workers in manufacturing of increased imports would have been only –734,000 unionized workers if increased imports had affected basically educated unionized worker in a manner proportional to their relative importance in employment terms. The difference between the –1,232,000 and –734,000 figures, or –498,000 workers, is the estimate of the disproportionately adverse impact of increased imports on basically educated unionized workers.

19. Again, let x and y equal the hypothetical employment effects of increased imports on basically educated union and nonunion workers, respectively, if the total decrease in the employment of basically educated workers associated with increased imports in 1987–97 (–1,055,000 plus –4,324,000 = –5,379,000; see table 5.7) is distributed in the same ratio as the total number of basically educated union to nonunion workers employed in manufacturing in 1987, namely, 0.43 (see table 5.5). Solving the two equations, $x/y = 0.43$ and $x + y = -5,379,000$, yields values for x and y of –1,617,000 and –3,762,000, respectively. The difference between the calculated value for basically educated union workers in table 5.7 (–1,055,000) and the hypothetical value for basically educated ones (–1,617,000) is +562,000.

Table 5.7 Estimated employment changes by education level and union status associated with changes in domestic spending, imports, exports, and labor coefficients, 1977–87 and 1987–97 (thousands of workers)

Education level and union status	Domestic spending	Imports	Exports	Labor coefficient	Other factors	Total
Manufactured goods						
Basically educated union workers						
1977–87	569	−1,232	156	86	−2,132	−2,553
1987–97	1,193	−1,055	−665	−306	−410	−1,243
Basically educated nonunion workers						
1977–87	1,164	−480	163	−1,388	635	94
1987–97	4,455	−4,324	197	−867	615	76
More-educated union workers						
1977–87	209	−121	52	−10	−237	−107
1987–97	981	−997	242	22	−159	89
More-educated nonunion workers						
1977–87	1,483	−332	149	−43	372	1,629
1987–97	2,947	−2,758	1,078	202	248	1,716
Traded goods and services						
Basically educated union workers						
1977–87	376	−683	265	−347	−2,715	−3,104
1987–97	84	−29	−550	−351	−646	−1,492
Basically educated nonunion workers						
1977–87	285	−48	854	−3,057	2,449	483
1987–97	2,056	−1,932	237	−623	−215	−477
More-educated union workers						
1977–87	111	−16	163	10	−269	−1
1987–97	−286	179	431	−286	−8	30
More-educated nonunion workers						
1977–87	1,798	−491	662	77	1,761	3,807
1987–97	4,321	−4,104	1,770	−11	4,061	6,037

Source: Author's calculations.

nonunion workers is +197,000. Following the same procedure used in estimating hypothetical effects of imports yields a hypothetical value for the expected number of basically educated union workers on the export side of −141,000 and basically educated nonunion workers of −327,000, because the employment ratio of basically educated union to nonunion workers in 1987 was 0.43.

Thus, the disproportionately adverse employment treatment on the export side of basically educated union workers in the 1987–97 decade was –524,000 (–665,000 minus –141,000). This number does not quite offset the measure of the disproportionately more favorable treatment of basically educated union workers compared with nonunion workers on the import side, namely, +562,000. The net disproportionately favorable employment effect of imports plus exports on basically educated unionized workers of 38,000 (562,000 minus 524,000) is equal to only about 9 percent of the –410,000 impact of "other factors" on the employment of basically educated unionized workers during the 1987–97 decade.

As was mentioned above, still another contrast with the earlier period is the statistically significant evidence that more-educated union workers in manufacturing in the 1987–97 period fared disproportionately adversely in employment-change terms from increased imports than more-educated nonunion workers (see table 5.5). Using the methodology followed in estimating such a number on the import side for the 1977–87 period, the extent of the disproportionately adverse effect of increased imports on more-educated workers is equal to –424,000 more-educated union workers.[20]

In addition to the information revealed about the relative importance of changes in imports and exports in accounting for any disproportionately adverse or less favorable impact on union workers, tables 5.6 and 5.7 also indicate the relative importance of the other independent variables on the changes in employment. For example, another relationship of interest is the association between changes in labor coefficients and changes in union versus nonunion employment.

One important finding with regard to this issue is that in the 1977–87 period, union workers fared much better compared with nonunion workers in terms of the employment-displacing effects of the decreases in labor coefficients. In manufacturing (see table 5.6), for example, the negative employment impact of the labor-coefficient decline in this period is only –17,000 jobs for union workers compared with –661,000 for nonunion workers, a ratio of 0.03—relative to an overall employment ratio of union to nonunion workers of 0.61 in 1977. Again, however, the 1987–97 period relationship is quite different. In this period, the employment displacement impact ratio was 0.31, compared with an employment ratio in 1987 of 0.33, thus indicating that the fall in labor coefficients affected union and nonunion workers in approximate proportion to their employment numbers in 1987.

---

20. In this case, the two equations are $x/y = 0.18$ and $x + y = -3,755,000$, so that $x = -573,000$ more-educated union workers and $y = -3,182,000$ more-educated nonunion workers. Therefore, the difference between the number of more-educated unionists in manufacturing reported for imports in table 5.7 for the 1987–97 period (–997,000) and number estimated above (–573,000) is –424,000.

In summary, the main conclusion to be drawn from this chapter is that factors other than simply changes in imports and exports mainly "explain" the extensive deunionization during the 1977–97 period. In the 1977–87 decade, the largest group of union workers in manufacturing, namely, those with 12 or fewer years of education, did face considerably larger employment-displacing import pressures relative to nonunion workers with the same educational background than would be expected from the relative importance of these two groups in the manufacturing labor force.

However, the opposite relationship held in the 1987–97 period. Yet export increases in this decade are also unexpectedly associated with an absolute decrease (rather than increase) in the employment of basically educated union workers. I speculate that the effect of other factors positively correlated with export increases, such as increased foreign direct investment and outsourcing, may account for this relationship and emphasize the need for more complex econometric models to investigate this issue. Still, deunionization among basically educated workers is mainly associated with factors not directly related to either import or export changes or the other independent variables in the regression equation but measured in the constant term in this equation.

6

Conclusions

Main Findings

It is difficult to exaggerate the seriousness of the organizational setback suffered by the US union movement in the last quarter of the 20th century. Whereas the proportion of workers who were members of unions rose in the 1950s and 1960s (though not as rapidly as in the 1930s and 1940s), the share of the labor force belonging to unions began to decline in the early 1970s.

This deunionization took the form not just of a fall in the percentage of the labor force that was unionized (the definition of deunionization used in this study) but also of an absolute decline in the number of union members. A striking statistic is the decline in the number of basically educated (12 or fewer years of schooling) unionized workers in manufacturing activities—a key group in the labor movement—by 3.8 million, or 63 percent, during the entire 1977–97 period and by 2.6 million, or 43 percent, just between 1977 and 1987.

The main contribution of this study is to size up provisionally the contributors to the decline in US unions. We find that global forces, often mentioned as an important contributor, play only a modest quantitative role. Their impact is, however, somewhat larger for basically educated (blue-collar) workers than for others. And the medium through which basically educated unionists were pressured changed during the period being studied; it was imports for most of the 1980s and exports in the 1990s (export markets are extremely competitive, and exports are closely related to foreign direct investment; both can threaten unionization).

We also find that other familiar deunionization suspects—such as the temporal shift in production toward less unionized service sectors and the less-unionized South—play at best a modest role in explaining the decline in unionization rates. The decline is ubiquitous, in all sectors and regions, suggesting deep fundamental sources such as growing employer opposition, unfavorable legislative trends, and declining worker trust in union institutions.

As this and other studies point out, during the 1977–97 period the proportion of unionized workers declined within all major product groupings, namely, primary-product industries, construction, manufacturing, and services. At a more detailed industry level, the main exception to the downward trend was in services largely carried out by federal, state, and local governments, such as public administration and educational services, in which the education levels of the workers were relatively high. In these sectors, the share of unionized workers either increased or remained roughly the same during the period.

Unionization rates also fell among both basically educated and more-educated workers (13 or more years) in all the major product categories, although much less for the latter group of workers. The overall declines from 1977 to 1997 were from 28.5 to 14.3 percent for basically educated workers and 18.6 to 13.4 percent for more-educated ones. The absolute number of unionized workers with 13 or more years of schooling actually increased in primary-product production, construction, and services, though not in manufacturing.

Still another indication of the pervasiveness of the deunionization is the decline in union membership by at least 50 percent in all regions of the country between 1977 and 1997. As with the national data, within-industries declines in unionization rates dominated shifts in the employment structure across industries in each region. There is some evidence, however, from my structural analysis that the South gained in total employment and unionization rates from a shift of such industries as transportation equipment and electric and electronic products from the North to the South.

Deunionization had a comparatively small effect on the earnings premium of union over nonunion workers. The ratio of the average weekly earnings of union members to nonunion workers fell from 1.40 in 1977 to 1.32 in 1997 over all sectors and from 1.19 to 1.16 in manufacturing.

"Decomposition" is the first method I used to assess the sources of deunionization. As a result of algebraically dividing the decline the national unionization rate into "between-industries" and "within-industries" components, we find that only about 27 percent of the decrease in the national unionization rate between 1977 and 1987 and 11 percent of the decrease between 1987 and 1997 can be attributed to shifts in the industry distribution of union workers away from industries that were historically more unionized to those that were less unionized. The decline of the rate of unionization within almost all industries is the dominant factor accounting for the deunionization.

The same result holds with regard to primary-product industries and construction, manufacturing activities, and the services sector. (In the small number of industries making up the primary-product and construction industries, the change in the structure of union employment across industries had the effect of increasing the rate of unionization.) When this decomposition exercise is undertaken for manufacturing activities in each of nine regions of the United States separately for the 1977–87 and 1987–97 periods, within-industry declines in unionization rates again dominate shifts in the distribution of union workers among industries in accounting for changes in regional unionization rates.

Still another decomposition analysis aims to indicate the extent to which the national deunionization in manufacturing is affected by changes in unionization rates within the different regions of the United States versus a redistribution of national employment from more unionized to less unionized regions. Just as the other decomposition exercises indicate shifts in the distribution of workers between industries (either nationally or within regions) play a relatively small role in accounting for deunionization in manufacturing, this analysis also indicates only a small role for the redistribution of workers across regions in explaining the extent of overall deunionization. Although the gain in national employment shares in the South and West (where unionization rates are generally lower than the national average) at the expense of the Mid-Atlantic and Upper Midwest accounts for part of the decline in the national unionization rate, a general decline in unionization rates within all regions is the dominant explanatory factor.

Regression analysis makes up the main empirical part of the study. This empirical investigation is based on a theoretical analysis of the economic effects of major real-side economic forces that affected the US economy during the last quarter of the 20th century. The investigation primarily seeks to ascertain whether the employment effects of changes in the volume of imports or exports affected union workers compared with nonunion workers in a more adverse (or less favorable) manner than would be expected, given their relative importance in the workforce.

In addition to analytically reviewing the impact of increases in international trade and foreign direct investment on the degree of unionization, I consider the possible effects of rapid technological progress, the increase in the supply of more-educated workers, and shifts in consumer preferences that occurred during the study period. The analysis demonstrates how major economic forces that operated in the world economy during the last quarter of the 20th century provide a number of plausible explanations for the membership difficulties faced by US labor unions, given the initial distribution of union members across industries and among different skill groups.

Because these various real-side economic forces all influence domestic output, imports, exports (in constant dollars), and the number of union and nonunion workers employed, and because data by industry are available on these variables for the period, I utilize regression analysis to determine if changes in US trade (controlling for changes in other real-side economic factors) affect union versus nonunion employment in a differential manner.

More specifically, I investigate whether changes in imports and exports across industries are associated with changes in the ratio of union to nonunion workers that differ in a statistically significant sense from the ratio of union to nonunion workers employed in these industries. Furthermore, I ask, if this is so, whether these trade changes in themselves are important factors associated with the changes in the number of union versus nonunion workers.

The main finding from my regression analysis is that factors *other* than changes in trade account for most of the large decrease in the number of union relative to nonunion workers. These factors are not associated with the other independent variables included in the regression equation, namely, changes in the number of workers required to produce a unit of the different goods and services resulting from technological change or changes in relative factor prices and relative shifts in spending among these goods and services. Instead, the constant term in the regression equation, which measures the effect of factors omitted from the regression model, "explains" most of the deunionization.

This finding is consistent with the belief of labor unions and many labor economists that a shift across most industries in attitudes by employers and workers unfavorable to unions—coupled with the enactment of new antiunion legislation and the administration of existing labor laws in an antiunion manner—are the main factors in the deunionization.

Although changes in the volume of international trade were not the dominant factor in deunionization during either the 1977–87 or 1987–97 period, import increases during the 1977–87 period did more adversely affect the employment of basically educated union workers in manufacturing than that of basically educated nonunion workers. This statistically significant effect is equal to about one-quarter of the negative employment impact on basically educated union workers attributable to the "other factors" measured by the constant term. In contrast, during the 1987–97 decade, basically educated union workers in manufacturing fared less adversely in employment than did basically educated nonunion workers.

Also in this period, however, increases in exports of manufactured goods are associated in a statistically significant manner with an absolute decline in the employment of basically educated union workers— even though, as expected, export increases are associated with increases in the employment of basically educated nonunion workers as well as more-educated union and nonunion workers.

I suggest that this relationship may be the consequence of increased foreign direct investment and outsourcing of production activities that can be performed by less-skilled, low-wage labor, which represent responses to increased competition in export markets and the unfavorable shifts in attitudes toward unions by US firms. Of course, inaccurate data on relevant variables may also account for this result, and I stress the need for a more complex econometric model that measures more directly the various economic forces affecting international trade and employment.

Still another relationship that differs between the 1977–87 and 1987–97 periods is the employment-displacing impact of increased imports on more-educated union versus more-educated nonunion workers employed in the manufacturing sector. During the first period this impact was roughly proportional to their employment ratio in 1977. However, in the 1987–97 decade the displacement ratio from increased imports of unionized workers with 13 or more years of schooling to nonunionized workers with this level of education was greater than their 1987 employment ratio in a statistically significant manner. The employment-creating impact in manufacturing of increased exports on more-educated unionists versus more-educated nonunionists was roughly proportional to their importance in employment terms in both periods.

The Need for More Extensive
Worker Assistance Programs

Although this study finds that the increase in the openness of US markets is not the major factor contributing to deunionization in the United States, there is no doubt that deunionization has adversely affected the employment security and earnings levels of many workers, especially basically educated union members. Given the absence and decline of private workers' associations and representation—such as unions—much greater governmental efforts are needed to assist those who lose their jobs though no fault of their own.

These assistance programs should cover workers who have been displaced not only by deunionization pressure but also by a wide variety of other forces, such as technological change and natural disasters. The programs should involve more extensive retraining and job search resources, insurance to partly compensate for wage losses associated with new jobs, and broad governmental efforts in depressed communities aimed at attracting more dynamic industries and helping workers receive the education required by these industries. And the appropriate response by organized labor to deunionization would seem to be devoting more attention to explaining the benefits of unions to both employers and workers and to eliminating antiunion provisions from existing legislation.

The wage insurance program proposed by Lori Kletzer and Robert Litan (2001; also see Kletzer 2001) is especially appealing because it not only provides a safety net for economically vulnerable workers but also promotes economic efficiency by encouraging workers to accept a new job even if it pays less than a lost one. Workers displaced from a job they had held for a certain minimum period (e.g., two years) would have a significant share (e.g., 50 percent) of their lost earnings replaced for up to two years after the date the job was lost. Subsidized health insurance would also be provided.

By tying the program's benefits to reemployment and limiting its benefits to a period starting from the date of job loss, this wage insurance program would discourage workers from waiting until a few weeks before their unemployment payments are about to expire before seriously looking for a new job. Kletzer and Litan estimate that with a two-year insurance period, 50 percent replacement rate, and $10,000 annual cap, the cost of the program would have been about $3 billion in 1997, when the average unemployment rate was 4.9 percent.

The main theme of this book underscores the need for such comprehensive adjustment and skill-building programs rather than, as now exists, programs mainly directed at workers in particular types of industries (e.g., seriously injured import-competing industries) or specific types of jobs. We find that increased openness to trade with other countries plays only a modest role in US deunionization. Many workers not employed in trade-related activities have also been adversely affected by the decline in unionization. This decline of unions seems due mainly to fundamental changes in attitudes and institutions associated with increased economic competitiveness throughout the entire economy, including employer opposition and worker disenchantment.

Consequently, dealing effectively with the resulting economic hardships imposed on vulnerable workers requires a broad policy approach. Efforts that focus on assisting only particular groups of workers are likely to prove inadequate in dealing with the adjustment problems associated with the basic causes of deunionization. Similarly, unless opportunities are provided for workers to acquire the education and skills needed to succeed in a highly competitive economy, the long-run political support needed to sustain such an economy will fail to develop.

APPENDICES

Appendix A
Data Sources

National Data

Unionization rates, weekly earnings, and level of education (12 or fewer years of education and 13 or more years of education) for 1977, 1987, and 1997 by industry for individuals working at least 35 hours a week are from the monthly Current Population Survey (CPS) conducted by the US Census Bureau. For 1977, the data are from the May survey; for 1987 and 1997, they are extracted from the outward rotation files in the monthly surveys of these latter years. Because the top code threshold changes over the time period, median rather than mean weekly earnings are calculated. The earnings data are deflated by the Consumer Price Index and are in 1983 dollars. The industry classification system used for all years and for all data used in the study is a modified version of the 1983 Census Industry Code (CIC), which consists of 137 industries that mostly match 3-digit Standard Industrial Classification (SIC) industries for 1987 but include some 2-digit and 4-digit SIC codes.

Employment Data

Employment data are from the Office of Employment Projections in the Bureau of Labor Statistics (BLS) of the US Department of Labor and are available from BLS at www.bls.gov. Shipments and receipts (in service sectors) are from the Economic Census for 1977, 1987, and 1997 and are deflated (1987 = 100) with prices from the BLS Office of Employment Projections. Exports and imports of goods for 1977 and 1987 are available from the National Bureau of Economic Research at www.nber.org from a data set assembled by Robert Feenstra. The 1997 export and import figures for goods are from the 1997 Economic Census of the US Census Bureau, Core Business Statistics Series, table 1, Comparative Statistics for the United States (1987 SIC Basic): 1997 and 1992. The concordance steps followed by Feenstra were used to make the 1997 trade data comparable to his 1977 and 1987 figures and then were reclassified to a CIC basis. Exports and imports of services are based on the six-digit input-output tables for 1977, 1987, and 1997 prepared by the Bureau of Economic Analysis in the US Department of Commerce.

Regional Data

The monthly Current Population Survey includes state as well as national data on unionization. The states making up the nine regions are listed in a footnote to table 3.2. Employment data by state and industry are available from BLS at www.bls.gov.

Appendix B
List of Industries in the Database

Code[1]	Industries and SIC code equivalent[2]
	Primary products
1. 010, 011	Agricultural production, crops, and livestock (01, 02)
2. 020, 030	Landscape, horticultural, and agricultural services (078)
3. 040	Metal mining (10)
4. 041	Coal mining (12)
5. 042	Oil and gas extraction (13)
6. 050	Nonmetallic mining and quarrying, except fuel (14)
	Construction
7. 060[3,4]	Construction (15, 16, 17)
	Manufacturing
8. 100	Meat products (201)
9. 101	Dairy products (202)
10. 102	Canned, frozen, and preserved fruits and vegetables (203)
11. 110	Grain mill products (204)
12. 111	Bakery products (205)
13. 112	Sugar and confectionery products 206)
14. 120	Beverage industries (208)
15. 121	Miscellaneous food preparations and kindred products (207, 209)
16. 130	Tobacco manufactures (21)
17. 132	Knitting mills (225)
18. 140	Dyeing and finishing textiles, except woollen and knitted goods (226)
19. 141	Carpets and rugs (227)

(*Appendix B continues next page*)

Code[1]	Industries and SIC code equivalent[2]
20. 142	Yarn, thread, and fabric mills (221–224, 228)
21. 150	Miscellaneous textile mills
22. 151	Apparel and accessories, except knit (231–238)
23. 152	Miscellaneous fabricated textile products (239)
24. 160	Pulp, paper, and paperboard mills (261–263)
25. 161	Miscellaneous paper and pulp products (267)
26. 162	Paperboard containers and boxes (265)
27. 171	Newspaper, publishing, and printing (271)
28. 172	Printing, publishing, and allied industries, except newspapers (272–279)
29. 180	Plastics, synthetics, and resins (282)
30. 181	Drugs (283)
31. 182	Soaps and cosmetics (284)
32. 190	Paints, varnishes, and related products (285)
33. 191	Agricultural chemicals (287)
34. 192	Industrial and miscellaneous chemicals (281, 286, 289)
35. 200	Petroleum refining (291)
36. 201	Miscellaneous petroleum and coal products (295, 299)
37. 210, 211	Tires, inner tubes, other rubber products, and plastic footwear and belting (302–306)
38. 212	Miscellaneous plastic products (308)
39. 220	Leather tanning and finishing (311)
40. 221	Footwear, except rubber and plastic (313, 314)
41. 222	Leather products, except footwear (315–317, 319)
42. 230	Logging (241)
43. 231	Sawmills, planing mills, and millwork (242, 243)
44. 232	Wood buildings and mobile homes, miscellaneous wood products (245, 244, 249)
45. 242	Furniture and fixtures (25)
46. 250	Glass and glass products (321–323)
47. 251	Cement, concrete, gypsum, and plaster products (324, 327)
48. 252	Structural clay products (325)
49. 261	Pottery and related products (326)
50. 262	Miscellaneous nonmetallic mineral and stone products (328, 329)
51. 270	Blast furnaces, steelworks, rolling and finishing mills (331)
52. 271	Iron and steel foundries (332)
53. 272	Primary aluminum industries (3334, part 334, 3353–3355, 3363, 3365)
54. 280	Other primary metal industries (3331, 3339, part 334, 3351, 3356, 3357, 3364, 3366, 3369, 339)
55. 281	Cutlery, hand tools, and general hardware (342)
56. 282	Fabricated structural metal products (344)
57. 290	Screw machine products (345)
58. 291	Metal forgings and stampings (346)
59. 292	Ordnance (292)

Code[1]	Industries and SIC code equivalent[2]
60. 300	Miscellaneous fabricated metal products (341, 343, 347, 349)
61. 310	Engines and turbines (351)
62. 311	Farm machinery and equipment (352)
63. 312	Construction and material-handling machines (353)
64. 320	Metalworking machinery (354)
65. 321	Office and accounting machines (3578, 3579)
66. 322	Computers and related equipment (3571–3577)
67. 331	Machinery, except electrical, n.e.c.[5] (355, 356, 358, 359)
68. 340	Household appliances (363)
69. 341	Radio, TV, and communication equipment (365, 366)
70. 342	Electrical machinery, equipment, and supplies, n.e.c.[5] (361, 362, 364, 367, 369)
71. 351	Motor vehicles and motor vehicle equipment (371)
72. 352	Aircraft and parts (372)
73. 360	Ship- and boat-building and repairing (373)
74. 361	Railroad locomotives and equipment (374)
75. 361, 392	Guided missiles, space vehicles, and parts; not specified manufacturing industries (376)
76. 370	Cycles and miscellaneous transportation equipment (375, 379)
77. 371	Scientific and controlling instruments (381, 382 except 3827)
78. 372	Medical, dental, and optical instruments and supplies (3827, 384, 385)
79. 380	Photographic equipment and supplies (386)
80. 381.	Watches, clocks, and clockwork-operated devices (387)
81. 390, 391	Toys, amusements, and sporting goods (394); miscellaneous manufacturing industries (39 except 394)

Services

82. 400	Railroads (40)
83. 401, 402[3,4]	Bus services and urban transit (41 except 412); taxicab services (412)
84. 410, 411[3,4]	Trucking services (421, 423); warehousing and storage (422)
85. 412	US Postal Service (43)
86. 420	Water transportation (44)
87. 421	Air transportation (45)
88. 422[3,4]	Pipelines, except natural gas (46)
89. 432[3,4]	Services incidental to transportation (47)
90. 440[3,4]	Radio and television broadcasting and cable (483, 484)
91. 441,442[3,4]	Telephone communications (481); telegraph and miscellaneous communication services (482, 489)
92. 450	Electric power and light (491)
93. 451,452[4]	Gas and steam supply systems (492, 496); electric and gas, and other combinations (493)
94. 470[3,4]	Water supply and irrigation (494, 497)
95. 471[3,4]	Sanitary services (495)

(Appendix B continues next page)

Code[1]	Industries and SIC code equivalent[2]
96. 500–571[3,4]	Wholesale trade (50, 51)
97. 580–691, ex. 641[3,4]	Retail trade (52–59 except 58)
98. 641[3,4]	Eating and drinking places (58)
99. 700–710 ex. 702[3,4]	Banking and finance (60, 62, 67)
100. 702[3,4]	Credit institutions, n.e.c.[5] (61)
101. 711	Insurance (63,64)
102. 712[3,4]	Real estate (65)
103. 721	Advertising (731)
104. 722[3,4]	Services to dwellings and other buildings (734)
105. 731[3]	Personnel supply services (736)
106. 732 [3]	Computer and data-processing services (737)
107. 740[3,4]	Detective and protective services (7381, 7382)
108. 741	Business services, n.e.c.[5] (732, 733, 735, 7382–7389)
109. 742[3,4]	Automotive rental and leasing (751)
110. 750[3,4]	Automotive parking and car washes (752, 7542)
111. 751[3,4]	Automotive repair and related services (753, 7549)
112. 752, 760	Electrical and miscellaneous repair shops (76)
113. 761[3,4]	Personal services, private households (88)
114. 762, 770[3,4]	Hotels, motels, and lodging places (701, 702, 703, 704)
115. 771, 790[3,4]	Laundry, cleaning, and garment services (721 except part 7219)
116. 772[3,4]	Beauty shops (723)
117. 780[3,4]	Barber shops (724)
118. 781, 782, 791[3,4]	Funeral services and crematories (726); shoe repair shops (725): dressmaking shops; miscellaneous personal services (722, 729)
119. 800	Theaters and motion pictures (781–783, 792)
120. 801[3,4]	Video tape rental (784)
121. 802, 810[3,4]	Bowling centers (793); miscellaneous entertainment and recreational services (791, 794, 799)
122. 812[3,4]	Offices and clinics of physicians (801, 803)
123. 820, 821, 822, 820[3,4]	Offices and clinics of dentists (802), chiropractors (8041), optometrists (8042), and health practitioners, n.e.c.[5] (8043, 8049)
124. 831[3,4]	Hospitals (806)
125. 832, 840[3,4]	Nursing and personal care facilities (805); health services, n.e.c.[5] (807,808, 809)
126. 841[3]	Legal services (81)
127. 842, 850[3]	Elementary and secondary schools (821); colleges and universities (822)
128. 851, 852 860[3,4]	Vocational schools (824); libraries (823); and educational services, n.e.c.[5] (829)
129. 861[3,4]	Job training and rehabilitation services (833)

Code[1]	Industries and SIC code equivalent[2]
130. 862, 863, 870[3,4]	Child day care services and family child care homes (835); residential care facilities, without nursing (836)
131. 871[3,4]	Social services, n.e.c.[5](832, 839)
132. 872[3,4]	Museums, art galleries, and zoos (84)
133. 873, 880, 881[3,4]	Membership organizations, labor unions, religious organizations (86)
134. 882	Engineering, architectural, and surveying services (871)
135. 890	Accounting, auditing, and bookkeeping services (871)
136. 891,892, 893[3]	Research, development, and testing services (873); management and public relations services (874); miscellaneous professional and related services (899)
137. 900–932[3,4]	Public administration (91–97)

1. 1983 Industry Classification Codes (3-digit) of Current Population Survey.
2. 1987 Standard Industrial Classification Code.
3. Excluded from 1977–87 regression data set.
4. Excluded from 1987–97 regression data set.
5. n.e.c. = not elsewhere classified.

References

Baldwin, Robert E., and Glen G. Cain. 2000. Shifts in Relative U.S. Wages: The Role of Trade, Technology, and Factor Endowments. *Review of Economics and Statistics* 82, no. 4: 580–95.

Cline, William R. 1997. *Trade and Income Distribution*. Washington: Institute of International Economics.

Deardorff, Alan, and Robert M. Stern, eds. 1994. *The Stolper-Samuelson Theorem: A Golden Jubilee*. Ann Arbor: University of Michigan Press.

Dickens, William, and Jon Leonard. 1985. Accounting for the Decline in Union Membership, 1950–1980. *Industrial and Labor Relations Review* 38, no. 3 (April): 323–34.

Farber, Henry S., and Alan B. Krueger. 1992. *Union Membership in the United States: The Decline Continues*. NBER Working Paper 4216. Cambridge, MA: National Bureau of Economic Research.

Freeman, Richard B. 1988. Concentration and Expansion: The Divergence of Private Sector and Public Sector Unionism in the United States. *Journal of Economic Perspectives* 2, no. 2 (spring): 63–88.

Kester, Anne Y., ed. 1992. *Behind the Numbers: U.S. Trade in the World Economy*. Washington: National Academy Press.

Kletzer, Lori G. 2001. *Job Loss from Imports: Measuring the Costs*. Washington: Institute for International Economics.

Kletzer, Lori G., and Robert E. Litan. 2001. *Prescription to Reduce Job Anxiety*. International Economics Policy Brief PB01-2. Washington: Institute for International Economics.

Lipsey, Robert E. Forthcoming. Home and Host Country Effects of FDI. In *Challenges to Globalization*, ed. Robert E. Baldwin and L. Alan Winters. Chicago: University of Chicago Press.

Reder, Melvin W. 1988. The Rise and Fall of Unions: The Public Sector and the Private. *Journal of Economic Perspectives* 2, no. 2 (spring): 89–110.

Rodrik, Dani. 1997. *Has Globalization Gone Too Far?* Washington: Institute for International Economics.

Slaughter, Matthew J. 2000. What Are the Results of Product-Price Studies and What Can We Learn from Their Differences? In *The Impact of International Trade on Wages*, ed: Robert C. Feenstra. Chicago: University of Chicago Press.

Index

adjustment assistance programs, 4, 69–70
agricultural products
  demand shifts and unionization rates, 31
  industry effects on national unionization, 18
agriculture, trade effects on employment, 40, 45
air traffic controllers' strike, 2
algebraical decomposition of unionization rates. *See* decomposition of unionization rates
analytical review of economic factor effects. *See* economic factors; *specific factors*
antiunionism. *See* employer attitudes toward unions; government attitudes toward unions; worker attitudes toward unions
apparel and textile sector, industry effects on regional unionization in manufacturing, 20, 22
auto industry, trade effects on employment, 39n

basically educated workers. *See also* educational level
  demand shifts and unionization rates, 31, 31n, 34
  earning levels and ratios, 11–13, 12t, 34–35
  employment changes and ratios, 50–51t, 54–57, 56n, 69
  median labor coefficient, 34, 34n
  national unionization rate trends, 4, 5, 9, 10, 65, 66
  services sector labor coefficients, 31, 31n
  supply of as factor, 4, 28, 32–34
  technology effects on unionization rates, 4, 27, 30–31, 33

trade effects on employment
  conclusions, 68
  overview, 4
  results, 45–46, 50–51t, 52, 54–57, 56n, 57n
  statistical model, 39
  summary statistics, 42, 43t, 44t, 45
  total employment effects, 59–64, 60n, 61t, 62n
trade effects on unionization rates, 5, 28–29, 29n, 33
unionized workers by product sector and educational level, 8t, 9t, 65, 66
worker assistance program needs, 69
"between-industries" effects. *See* industry effects
"between-regions" effects. *See* regional effects
blue-collar workers. *See* basically educated workers
Bureau of Economic Analysis, data sources, 40, 74
Bureau of Labor Statistics, data sources, 1n, 40, 73–74

Census Bureau
  data sources, 1n, 40, 73, 74
  product value reporting, 39n
Census Industry Codes (CIC)
  data sources, 73, 74
  industries list, 75–79t
collective bargaining laws. *See* labor laws
Commerce Department
  data sources, 40, 74
  product value reporting, 39n
communication costs and technology, 27, 29
competition
  and deunionization trends, 2, 65

Other Publications from the Institute for International Economics

*= out of print

POLICY ANALYSES IN INTERNATIONAL ECONOMICS Series

31 **The Economic Opening of Eastern Europe***
John Williamson
May 1991   ISBN 0-88132-186-9

32 **Eastern Europe and the Soviet Union in the World Economy***
Susan M. Coffins and Dani Rodrik
May 1991   ISBN 0-88132-157-5

33 **African Economic Reform: The External Dimension***   Carol Lancaster
June 1991   ISBN 0-88132-096-X

34 **Has the Adjustment Process Worked?***
Paul R. Krugman
October 1991   ISBN 0-88132-116-8

35 **From Soviet disUnion to Eastern Economic Community?***
Oleh Havrylyshyn and John Williamson
October 1991   ISBN 0-88132-192-3

36 **Global Warming The Economic Stakes***
William R. Cline
May 1992   ISBN 0-88132-172-9

37 **Trade and Payments After Soviet Disintegration***   John Williamson
June 1992   ISBN 0-88132-173-7

38 **Trade and Migration: NAFTA and Agriculture***   Philip L. Martin
October 1993   ISBN 0-88132-201-6

39 **The Exchange Rate System and the IMF: A Modest Agenda**   Morris Goldstein
June 1995   ISBN 0-88132-219-9

40 **What Role for Currency Boards?**
John Williamson
September 1995   ISBN 0-88132-222-9

41 **Predicting External Imbalances for the United States and Japan***William R. Cline
September 1995   ISBN 0-88132-220-2

42 **Standards and APEC: An Action Agenda***
John S. Wilson
October 1995   ISBN 0-88132-223-7

43 **Fundamental Tax Reform and Border Tax Adjustments***   Gary Clyde Hufbauer
January 1996   ISBN 0-88132-225-3

44 **Global Telecom Talks: A Trillion Dollar Deal***
Ben A. Petrazzini
June 1996   ISBN 0-88132-230-X

45 **WTO 2000: Setting the Course for World Trade**   Jeffrey J. Schott
September 1996   ISBN 0-88132-234-2

46 **The National Economic Council: A Work in Progress ***   I. M. Destler
November 1996   ISBN 0-88132-239-3

47 **The Case for an International Banking Standard**   Morris Goldstein
April 1997   ISBN 0-88132-244-X

48 **Transatlantic Trade: A Strategic Agenda***
Ellen L. Frost
May 1997   ISBN 0-88132-228-8

49 **Cooperating with Europe's Monetary Union**
C. Randall Henning
May 1997   ISBN 0-88132-245-8

50 **Renewing Fast Track Legislation*** I. M.Destle
September 1997   ISBN 0-88132-252-0

51 **Competition Policies for the Global Economy**
Edward M. Graham and J. David Richardson
November 1997   ISBN 0-88132 -249-0

52 **Improving Trade Policy Reviews in the Worl Trade Organization**   Donald Keesing
April 1998   ISBN 0-88132-251-2

53 **Agricultural Trade Policy: Completing the Reform** Timothy Josling
April 1998   ISBN 0-88132-256-3

54 **Real Exchange Rates for the Year 2000**
Simon Wren Lewis and Rebecca Driver
April 1998   ISBN 0-88132-253-9

55 **The Asian Financial Crisis: Causes, Cures, and Systemic Implications** Morris Goldstein
June 1998   ISBN 0-88132-261-X

56 **Global Economic Effects of the Asian Currency Devaluations**
Marcus Noland, LiGang Liu, Sherman Robinson, and Zhi Wang
July 1998   ISBN 0-88132-260-1

57 **The Exchange Stabilization Fund: Slush Money or War Chest?**   C. Randall Henning
May 1999   ISBN 0-88132-271-7

58 **The New Politics of American Trade: Trade, Labor, and the Environment**
I. M. Destler and Peter J. Balint
October 1999   ISBN 0-88132-269-5

59 **Congressional Trade Votes: From NAFTA Approval to Fast Track Defeat**
Robert E. Baldwin and Christopher S. Magee
February 2000   ISBN 0-88132-267-9

60 **Exchange Rate Regimes for Emerging Markets: Reviving the Intermediate Option**
John Williamson
September 2000   ISBN 0-88132-293-8

61 **NAFTA and the Environment: Seven Years Later**   Gary Clyde Hufbauer, Daniel Esty, Diana Orejas, Luis Rubio, and Jeffrey J. Schott
October 2000   ISBN 0-88132-299-7

62 **Free Trade between Korea and the United States?** Inbom Choi and Jeffrey J. Schott
April 2001   ISBN 0-88132-311-X

63 **New Regional Trading Arrangements in the Asia Pacific?**
Robert Scollay and John P. Gilbert
May 2001   ISBN 0-88132-302-0

64 **Parental Supervision: The New Paradigm for Foreign Direct Investment and Development**
Theodore H. Moran
August 2001   ISBN 0-88132-313-6

WORKS IN PROGRESS

DISTRIBUTORS OUTSIDE THE UNITED STATES

**Australia, New Zealand,
and Papua New Guinea**
D.A. Information Services
648 Whitehorse Road
Mitcham, Victoria 3132, Australia
tel: 61-3-9210-7777
fax: 61-3-9210-7788
email: service@adadirect.com.au
http://www.dadirect.com.au

United Kingdom and Europe
(including Russia and Turkey)
The Eurospan Group
3 Henrietta Street, Covent Garden
London WC2E 8LU England
tel: 44-20-7240-0856
fax: 44-20-7379-0609
http://www.eurospan.co.uk

Japan and the Republic of Korea
United Publishers Services, Ltd.
KenkyuSha Bldg.
9, Kanda Surugadai 2-Chome
Chiyoda-Ku, Tokyo 101 Japan
tel: 81-3-3291-4541
fax: 81-3-3292-8610
email: saito@ups.co.jp
**For trade accounts only.
Individuals will find IIE books in
leading Tokyo bookstores.**

Thailand
Asia Books
5 Sukhumvit Rd. Soi 61
Bangkok 10110 Thailand
tel: 662-714-07402 Ext: 221, 222, 223
fax: 662-391-2277
email: purchase@asiabooks.co.th
http://www.asiabooksonline.com

Canada
Renouf Bookstore
5369 Canotek Road, Unit 1
Ottawa, Ontario KlJ 9J3, Canada
tel: 613-745-2665
fax: 613-745-7660
http://www.renoufbooks.com

India, Bangladesh, Nepal, and Sri Lanka
Viva Books Pvt.
Mr. Vinod Vasishtha
4325/3, Ansari Rd.
Daryaganj, New Delhi-110002
India
tel: 91-11-327-9280
fax: 91-11-326-7224
email: vinod.viva@gndel.globalnet.
ems.vsnl.net.in

Southeast Asia (Brunei, Cambodia,
China, Malaysia, Hong Kong, Indonesia,
Laos, Myanmar, the Philippines, Singapore,
Taiwan, and Vietnam)
Hemisphere Publication Services
1 Kallang Pudding Rd. #0403
Golden Wheel Building
Singapore 349316
tel: 65-741-5166
fax: 65-742-9356

**Visit our Web site at:
http://www.iie.com
E-mail orders to:
orders@iie.com**